AIR FRYER
easy everyday

AIR
FRYER
easy everyday

140 super-simple,
delicious recipes

Sam & Dom Milner
of RecipeThis

WHITE LION
PUBLISHING

Quarto

First published in 2024 by White Lion Publishing
an imprint of The Quarto Group.
One Triptych Place,
London,
SE1 9SH
United Kingdom
T (0)20 7700 6700
www.Quarto.com

A catalogue record for this book is available from the British Library.

HB ISBN 978 0 7112 9813 2
PB ISBN 978 0 7112 9814 9
Ebook ISBN 978 0 7112 9815 6

10 9 8 7 6 5 4 3 2 1

Designer: Georgie Hewitt
Project Editor & Food Stylist: Rebecca Woods
Photographer: Dan Jones
Prop Stylist: Faye Wears
Group Publishing Director: Denise Bates
Editorial Director: Nicky Hill
Senior Production Controller: Rohana Yusef
Air fryer icon illustrator: Renata Latipova
Printed in China

Key to symbols

Recipe is suitable for:

 Basket air fryer

 Dual air fryer

 Air fryer oven

Small air fryer

Notes

- All calorie counts are per serving where a recipe states "Serves" or per item when a recipe states "Makes"
- Metric and imperial measurements are given for all recipes, use one set only and not a mixture of both
- All tablespoons and teaspoons are level
- All milk should be whole/full-fat unless otherwise stated
- All eggs should be UK large eggs or US XL eggs, unless otherwise stated
- Be careful when handling raw chicken, never wash it and never use anything that has come into contact with it ie utensils and chopping boards, on cooked foods without washing them thoroughly first.
- When baking sweet treats, we recommend unsalted butter, and in savoury cooking salted butter. Unless otherwise stated, bring the butter to room temperature before using.
- Do refer to your air fryer manual, as they often operate differently and follow the manufacturer's safety guidelines.

Contents

WELCOME

We're Sam and Dom, and we love cooking with kitchen gadgets. We have been air frying for 12 years – long before it was a social media trend and long before there was the current huge range of air fryers on the market. Back then, you just had the Philips air fryer, which was much smaller than it is today, and people were using them for the basics, such as making homemade chips, warming up pastries or cooking frozen food. You couldn't cook a whole chicken in it, or any cakes larger than 15cm/6 inch. Today, people are using their air fryers for a much broader range of dishes, and there is a wider variety of air fryers to reflect the more diverse air frying community.

On meeting someone new with an air fryer, the first question is always "Which air fryer do you have?" Do you have the oven? Do you have the basket? Do you have the dual?

This got us thinking about a topic for our second air fryer cookbook. With the focus on easy everyday air fryer recipes, we decided to develop the recipes around the most popular styles of air fryers. Every recipe in this book has been tested in the basket, dual and air fryer oven, and we have provided guidance on how to adapt recipes to some other styles of air fryer.

But while the recipes will work in all the air fryers for which a symbol appears (check out the variations at the bottom of the pages), some recipes really wow us in a particular air fryer. With this in mind, you will see "hero" mentions. Look out for the hero mention for your type of air fryer, and why not start with those recipes?

We hope that you love these air fryer recipes as much as we do.

Sam & Dom x

understanding
air fryers

air fryer basics

WHAT IS AN AIR FRYER?

An air fryer is what I call my "magic machine", because every time I create a new recipe and push the air fryer to its new limits it feels like I have achieved magic. Cynics will tell you that an air fryer is just a small convection oven, but they are much more than that. Air fryers use powerful fans to circulate hot air around the food. Because they are much smaller than a standard oven, it means that they cook food much faster.

You can cook most things in an air fryer that you would usually cook in the oven, under the grill/broiler, in the microwave, the toaster, the sandwich maker, the deep fat fryer, the wok, and the cast iron casserole dish. Because air fryers replace so many other machines, you can save space in your kitchen by just having an air fryer and they can sit on your countertop.

10 REASONS WHY WE LOVE AIR FRYING

They cook more quickly Cooking the average whole chicken in the oven takes around 1¾ hours, plus a preheat. Yet the same chicken will cook in the air fryer in under an hour.

You don't need to preheat an air fryer It always feels like such an effort to preheat an oven and having to get it nice and hot before you start cooking. Yet with an air fryer it only requires a preheat on a handful of recipes, and even then it's only a couple of minutes.

There is no parboiling required I remember as a kid watching my mum cook roast potatoes. She would parboil the potatoes, before oven roasting them. The air fryer is much better; you peel and quarter the potatoes and toss them in oil and seasonings, then the air fryer does the hard work for you.

They use a lot less oil Cooking a whole chicken in the oven requires lots of butter under the skin, to stop it drying out, whereas in the air fryer a whole chicken needs just one tablespoon of olive oil.

Most are energy efficient I have a gadget attached to our smart meter that tells us how much electricity we are using. It will go red if we run the kettle and the microwave at the same time. Yet we can run four air fryers at once when recipe testing and it will stay at green.

They are easy to use I cannot think of an easier way to cook. There are so many easy recipes to follow, many with few ingredients – perfect for quickly prepping dinner, or for those who hate cooking.

They travel well Most motorhome and caravan owners we know have an air fryer. We have travelled many times with our air fryer and it makes keeping the holiday grocery costs down so much easier. (There's more about travelling with the air fryer on page 14.)

You can reduce the fat in your diet This is perfect if you are on a diet, suffer from high cholesterol or generally like eating healthily. You will find that for the average serving size for dinner in the air fryer, you will need just ¼ tablespoon of extra virgin olive oil.

You can leave the air fryer to it Imagine standing over a pan sautéing some onions. Then imagine placing them into the air fryer, leaving the room and only coming back when the air fryer beeps. In the Milner house, we love being able to put the food in the air fryer and leave it to it.

They are easier to clean than an oven Forget all those roasting tins that you have to scrub. Instead, there are plenty of accessories that make cleaning up quick and soak-free – most can just be popped in the dishwasher. Along with this, the air fryer itself just needs a quick wipe down with hot soapy water.

the air fryer range

We bought our first air fryer basket in 2012, upgraded to a bigger one in 2016, bought our first air fryer oven in 2019, also got our first multi cooker with air fryer function the same year and then jumped on the dual bandwagon in early 2023. They are like family, so we can't choose a favourite – we love them all. But if you want just one, hard-working machine, there are various things to consider.

ALL AIR FRYERS ARE DIFFERENT

This is the biggest consideration when you are deciding which air fryer to have in your kitchen. You walk into an electronics store and the salesperson tells you that you must have whichever one is popular at the time. It will either be the one that is selling best, or the one that they get a higher commission for.

And not all air fryers are the same. There are basket air fryers, some with extra-large baskets and some with tiny ones. There are dual air fryers with two drawers, or multi cookers with an air fryer function, air fryers with a crisper plate, others with a standard basket. There are air fryer ovens, or air fryer ovens with a rotisserie function, some have five shelves, some have four shelves. The combinations feel seemingly endless, and I am sure after that list I have overwhelmed you.

Well, it gets a little more complicated. Each brand will have different quirks, and some air fryers will be better than others – they all have different strengths and weaknesses. Just like choosing a television, or a phone or a washing machine, they all have pros and cons. As a result, it's not unheard of to make an inappropriate choice, hate your air fryer, then think air fryers are rubbish and wonder why everyone likes them so much!

That's why we're here to help. Throughout this chapter we are going to give you a crash course in air fryers, including the benefits of each type of air fryer, so that you can make the best choice for your first air fryer, or so that you have all the information for when you upgrade or add an extra air fryer to your kitchen.

Most importantly, we'll explain how the cooking time of your food may vary depending on which air fryer you have, and how to adapt the recipe you're following.

LET'S START WITH AIR FRYER BASKETS

The basket air fryer is the most common type of air fryer and the one that has been around the longest. First released by Philips in 2010 after a partnership with Fred Van Der Weij, continental Europe loved it! We bought our first one in 2012 and noticed at the time that only Germany and the Netherlands were taking it seriously. Today, most recipes you see online are written for cooking in the basket models.

In basket air fryers, food is placed into a perforated basket with a handle. This basket then clips into a larger drawer, which is inserted into the main unit with the heating element. The food is cooked quickly as the basket raises it up from the base of the drawer, meaning that air can circulate all around. There are usually deep indentations in the drawer base, which helps the air to circulate efficiently. To remove the food from the air fryer, you simply unclip the basket and lift it out of the drawer, then food can be tipped out of the basket directly onto plates.

When they were first introduced, air fryer baskets were much smaller and the food you could cook in them was more basic. (Forget roasting a whole chicken back in 2012.) But over the years, with many popular electronics brands competing, they have got bigger and better. For example, Philips started at about 4.2 litres/4.4 quart and now they have the XL which is 6.2 litres/ 6.5 quart and XXL which is the most powerful air fryer we have personally used and is 7.2 litres/7.6 quart, which is larger than most on the market.

but what sized air fryer basket should you get?

Cooking capacity is real area of confusion, and our readers often contact us about this. Like a slow cooker, air fryer size is given in units of

volume, not physical size. So when you read the air fryer specifications and it says 4.2 litres/4.4 quart, you may well wonder what that actually means in a real life cooking scenario.

Well, I have another way: I measure air fryers – both ones I use now and ones I have used in the past – and work out which size round baking pan will fit well in the basket. This gives me a better idea of what I can cook in the space (and helps me visualise it) and have a clearer idea about which sized air fryer I need in my kitchen. Although models do vary, I have found the below to be reasonably accurate:

2.0 litre/2.1 quart – 14cm/5½ inch
4.2 litre/4.4 quart – 16.5cm/6½ inch
5.5 litre/5.8 quart – 20cm/8 inch
6.2 litre/6.5 quart – 20cm/8 inch
7.2 litre/7.6 quart – 23cm/9 inch

You can use these baking pan sizes as a guide for buying accessories for your air fryer, such as silicone pans. We have sometimes found that the same-sized accessories fit two different sizes of air fryer because the volume difference is in the height of the basket, not the size of the base.

We find the 4.2 litre air fryer, known as "medium" is perfect for one to two people, although it won't hold a whole chicken. Instead, try our smaller piri piri poussin (see page 82).

We have both 5.5 litre and 6.2 litre XL air fryers in our home kitchen and they are perfect for two to four people – or for those who love whole chicken or want to cook a full meal in the air fryer.

The 7.2 litre XXL models are very spacious and ideal for a family of four. You can cook a larger chicken in them, as well as several portions of chips without it feeling overcrowded.

THE SINGLE DRAWER AIR FRYER

The single drawer air fryer has a similar shape and capacity to the basket models. The main difference is that instead of a perforated basket that sits inside the main drawer, these models have drawers with a flat base and a perforated crisper plate that sits inside the drawer. Like the basket, these plates raise up the food so that air can circulate underneath and food can crisp up. As there is no inset basket, the handle is attached to the drawer itself.

The bonus of this style of air fryer is the ability to remove the crisper plate so that you can cook dishes with lots of liquid (such as soups, sauces and curries) directly in the drawer, rather than having to transfer them to a silicone container, or similar. The drawer can essentially act as a saucepan, and as they are non-stick, they are easy to clean.

You can cook food with the plate (for dryer items that you want to crisp) or without (for saucier foods), or even use a combination of cooking styles by removing the crisper plate halfway through. For example, if you were cooking our root vegetable soup (see page 128), you would air fry the root vegetables with the crisper plate in place, then remove it before adding liquids. (It's worth noting that you can cook in this way in a standard basket air fryer too, but you will just need to transfer the vegetables to an air fryer accessory before adding the liquids to finish the cooking process.)

When purchasing an air fryer, opt for an air fryer with a removeable crisper plate if you plan to make a lot of recipes with liquids. And beware: if you are upgrading from a basket model to an air fryer with a crisper plate, the plate gets very hot, just like a heavy baking tray you have just removed from the oven. If you are used to tipping food straight out of the basket onto a plate, it is easy to forget that the crisper plate is loose and tip the red hot crisper plate onto your hand in the process. Use less of an angle when tipping, or use a kitchen utensil to remove the food.

For the recipes in this book, adapt as necessary. You will find that you don't have to transfer wet ingredients to silicone as you would if using the basket, and you'll likely not have to reduce the size of your accessories (or split them between drawers) as you would for the dual. And keep the crisper plate in unless directed to remove it in the recipe, because if the food is not raised up, it will take slightly longer to cook.

THE DUAL AIR FRYER

The dual air fryer has gained the most popularity in recent years and is like having two drawer air fryers in one. Forget just filling one drawer with food, you now have two, giving you much more space! Like the single drawer air fryers, the drawers have crisper plates and can be used as saucepans too when those are removed. All single drawer or basket air fryer recipes can be cooked in the dual, although the drawers are narrower and so the physical cooking spaces are smaller despite a larger capacity overall.

how does a dual air fryer differ from the others?

In terms of times and temperatures to use when air frying, the method of cooking in a dual is almost identical to single drawer or basket air fryers – you're simply cooking in two rectangular spaces rather than one square one, and you will have about 50 per cent more space, too.

The main advantage of the dual is that it gives you the scope to cook two totally different things at the same time, even at different temperatures and in different styles. For example, you can remove the crisper plate from one drawer and use it to make our saucy chicken curry (see page 191), while leaving the plate in the second drawer and using it to cook our Bombay potatoes (see page 159), which really opens up possibilities.

there are just a few considerations

The drawers are narrower than a basket so what you could fit in one basket, you might need to spread out over two drawers. For example, when cooking the lamb roast (see page 192) in a basket air fryer, we would cook the lamb in the centre of the basket, surrounded by the vegetables. In the dual drawers, you would add meat to one drawer and the veggies to the other. The time and temperature would be the same. Use personal judgement and divide food between the drawers if one seems too full.

Dividing the food may mean it cooks more quickly For example, if you are making the French fries (see page 154) and spread them between drawers, you will have less food in each drawer compared to making the full batch in one air fryer basket. Less food in each may mean it cooks more quickly, so do check the food a few minutes before the recipe states so that you don't overcook it.

Speed up the sides Sometimes when air frying, you can be cooking the main element of a dish, such as a piece of meat or fish, then waiting on the air fryer to finish before you can cook any accompaniments. With the dual, you can cook your veggies in one drawer and your meat in the other. For example, with our teriyaki duck noodles (see page 94) we can cook the veggie stir fry mix in one drawer, then the duck in the other.

The different function buttons Some dual air fryers have several functions, including air fry, bake and roast. Unless stated otherwise, recipes in this book always use the "air fry" button, as it produces the best results. But on machines with multiple functions, most "air fry" settings cook between 160–210ºC/320–410ºF. Therefore, if you need to cook at a lower heat (such as when melting butter or chocolate) you can use the "bake" function, which is much gentler.

"Match" is our favourite feature When we got our first dual air fryer, we fell in love with the "match" feature, which allows you to simultaneously set the same time and temperature for both drawers. It's perfect if two different foods require the same cooking time and temperature, or if you're simply dividing the same ingredients between both drawers.

"Sync" is our lazy feature If you are cooking two different foods with different cooking times, the "sync" feature let's you set the time and temperature for both drawers at the beginning, then staggers the start times so that they will finish cooking at the same time. This means that you don't need to come back into the kitchen to get the other drawer going.

Adapting is key There are so many different sized dual air fryers – from the smaller 7.6 litres/8 quart models to those with a larger 10 litre/10.5 quart capacity. You will need to buy air fryer accessories that comfortably fit the dimensions of your two drawers.

The dual air fryer is best for People who like variety. Before air frying, you would cook a soup in a saucepan, then turn the oven on for the part-baked bread rolls. Now you can cook the soup in one drawer and warm up the bread in the other.

THE FLEX DRAWER AIR FRYER

This is the rising star of air fryers – part dual, part single drawer air fryer, they offer the best of both worlds. They have one very large drawer (up to 9–10 litres/9.5–10.5 quart) with a removeable divider that can be slotted into the centre. This gives them the capability of cooking with two different temperature zones with the divider inserted, as you can in a dual. However, remove it and they become a very large version of a single drawer air fryer, with a crisper plate (or plates) that can be removed so it can serve as a very large saucepan, too. We love it for recipes like the lamb roast (see page 192) because, with the divider removed, it will accommodate a larger lamb joint.

If you are lucky enough to have one of these models, you can follow the dual instructions, because it too has a crisper plate that can be removed so you won't need to transfer wet ingredients into containers. However, you will find that you are also unlikely to need to split ingredients between two different drawers, as you will have one very large capacity drawer to use, and so cake tins, for example, will fit at the sizes stated in the recipe.

AIR FRYER OVEN

This is the third type of air fryer we primarily focus on in this book. If you like cooking with an oven, an air fryer oven is like a mini version, with shelves rather than a basket or drawer, although unlike an oven, you can cook directly on the shelves without any bakeware. If you want lots of space, they are much bigger than a basket or dual air fryer, and many models also have an amazing rotisserie accessory. We love the air fryer oven so much that we have a chapter dedicated to them, starting on page 60.

LET'S TALK SMALL AIR FRYERS

You may have seen the small basket air fryers when browsing. They look tiny beside the XL alternatives, and even smaller when beside a dual air fryer.

A small air fryer is often one-third the size of an XL air fryer or one-fifth the capacity of a large dual air fryer. Typically a small air fryer is 2 litres/ 2.1 quart but we have seen them smaller.

Despite their diminutive size and lower wattage, they still carry the same cook time as more powerful, larger air fryers. This is because they have a smaller volume and so require less power to warm up and there will be less food to cook.

so why would you want such a small air fryer?

Cooking for one These small air fryers were originally made for one person. The idea is that if you just want to cook a single pork steak with some vegetables, or a chicken breast rather than a whole chicken, you can.

Just for chips I have met many people who just use their small air fryer for chips. It's simply a deep fat fryer replacement and they have no interest in anything else. In which case this size is perfect.

travelling with the air fryer

A small air fryer is perfect for travelling with as it's compact and doesn't take up much room. It fits nicely in the boot of your car, is easy to take to a holiday cottage, plus its low wattage is perfect for using on campsites.

We have travelled to Spain many times with our air fryer and it makes cooking so much easier. I can buy local food, then cook it in the air fryer for dinner in our self-catering accommodation. Because we like to drive to our destination, a smaller air fryer takes up a lot less room in the car, and I can still avoid the holiday apartment oven. Plus, to save money on eating out, a small air fryer is also good for pasties, toasties and a quick portion of chips.

During the many times we have stayed at campsites, we have found that it's very easy to blow a fuse and trip the electric. Then you have to head to the campsite's reception with a sheepish look on your face, apologising as they reconnect the electric for you. This will easily happen if you use a bigger air fryer, but small 2 litre/2.1 quart air fryers are low watt and subsequently more campsite friendly. If you are worried about power supply on campsites, I recommend going for an air fryer under 1000 wattage and these are usually under 2 litres/2.1 quart in capacity.

Chicken drumsticks from air fryer to air fryer

Now that I have run through the different types of air fryers, let me talk you through cooking chicken drumsticks in different air fryers.

First we like to flavour them with one of our marinades from page 37. Then, we place the drumsticks in the air fryers as shown below.

01 **Air fryer basket (or single drawer)** Place three chicken drumsticks from left to right and one along the bottom.

02 **Air fryer dual** Instead of left to right, lay them top to bottom as the dual is narrow and tall vs a square basket. You can also double batch and cook four in each drawer.

03 **Small air fryer basket** Simply space two chicken drumsticks in the small area you have available. Or swap two medium drumsticks for four small ones to fit the air fryer size.

04 **Air fryer oven** Place four drumsticks on an air fryer oven shelf/rack. If you are cooking just one shelf of chicken drumsticks, you can use any of the shelves, because the air circulates so well it doesn't affect the cooking time.

In a basket or dual air fryer, we will cook them at 180°C/360°F for 17 minutes (turning them over after 10 minutes), or until the drumsticks reach an internal temperature of 70°C/160°F or above.

If we are cooking in an air fryer oven, preheat for 2 minutes, then cook them on a single shelf for 21 minutes (turning them over after 10 minutes), or until cooked through. If you are cooking two shelves of drumsticks, cook them for a total of 26 minutes, switching the shelves around halfway through cooking.

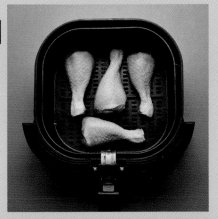

cooking for one

We have many air fryer readers who are cooking for one: from the older person living alone and the single professional to students heading to university and becoming independent for the first time. The first question they ask us, is "How easy are air fryer recipes to adapt for one person?" and my first response is always that the air fryer is made for YOU! Unlike a family, you don't need two air fryers or a dual for full meals, and it's easy to batch and make meals ahead so that it doesn't feel like you're cooking all the time just for yourself.

I wish the air fryer was about when my Grandma was widowed 31 years ago. She didn't like cooking and would have loved warming up her favourite meals in it. I also love watching our best mate with it, who is a single working professional who works unsociable shifts and loves how easy it is.

If you're cooking for one, how should you adapt these air fryer recipes? Which are best for one person? What freezes well, and are you stuck eating the same kind of food all the time?

how to convert recipes

For many of the recipes in this book that serve four people, you can divide the ingredients by four and make it into a recipe to serve one. I do this frequently with Bombay potatoes because the rest of my household doesn't care for Indian food. I can quarter the ingredients and keep the same time and temperature. The same goes for a meal like corned beef hash (see page 50) – I simply halve the ingredients and make it for one.

While it is often easy to reduce the quantities (in proportion) for a regular meal or side dish, if you wanted to reduce a baking recipe, we suggest that you follow our dual adaptations, which provide options for smaller cooking accessories. For example, our sprinkle cake (see page 212), can be cooked in four mini tins to fit the dual drawers, so you can simply quarter the recipe and make just one mini cake (which serves two) and enjoy it over a couple of days!

When adapting the recipes, be aware that if you have much less food in the air fryer, it may cook more quickly as the air can circulate more freely. Therefore, cooking times stated in the recipes may be slightly too long, and you'll need to keep an eye on the food, especially towards the end of the cooking time.

Top tips

Choose an XL air fryer basket (such as a 5.5 litre/5.8 quart air fryer capacity) for full meals. This is a very useful size for fitting a piece of protein, such as a turkey steak, alongside a portion of potatoes and vegetables, and cooking everything together in the same basket. (See our turkey dinner for one on page 92.)

If you have a mini air fryer (such as the 2 litre/2.1 quart) you can make our poussin recipe (see page 82) and cook the fries at the same time.

Make ahead and freeze It can get a bit boring when you are cooking for one and dinner is often a single chicken breast cooked in the air fryer. Instead, we love making chicken bags to add exciting flavours. Chicken is marinated in heavy duty freezer bags, then frozen in portions. We have a choice of seven different marinades (see page 37) so you can prepare a variety and make mealtimes more fun.

Batch cook There are lots of recipes in this book that you can batch cook and freeze in single portions, then air fry later. Some of our favourites include chilli con carne (see page 55), sweet potato and chickpea curry (see page 130), or sausages and peppers (see page 105).

Make a smaller portion See opposite for how to adapt larger recipes to serve one – or just halve a standard "serves four" recipe to serve two people so that you have lunch ready for the next day!

let's talk air fryer accessories

I have bought many air fryer accessories over the years – some have been amazing, some have been okay and some have been useless. It's a learning curve, and as you buy accessories, you will see which ones work for you. In our accessories section, I will share which types of air fryer accessories we find useful, and which of our recipes they are used in.

WHY DO YOU EVEN NEED AIR FRYER ACCESSORIES?

You need air fryer accessories just like you need accessories for a standard oven. In the oven you would cook with a range of metal, ceramic or silicone bakeware, and the same applies to cooking in the air fryer.

There is a huge range of air fryer accessories available, but we don't want you wasting money, so the ones featured here are only those that we personally used while writing the recipes for this book.

You can use any accessory brand you like, you just need to make sure that what you have fits your air fryer size and that you're not going to slow down the cooking process too much. For example, tightly wrapping food in foil, or adding foil over food too soon (to stop the browning), can slow down the cooking time, as can very using thick silicone or glass, so plan this into your cooking time.

We have found some of our favourite accessories when we were not expecting to. Charity shops that sell bric a brac, supermarkets with good "home" departments that we wander into when doing our weekly food shop, or department stores are all great sources. The bakeware aisle is a good source for small roasting tins that fit your air fryer oven, fun coloured silicone muffin cups or different sized foil trays.

WHAT ACCESSORIES CAN YOU USE IN THE AIR FRYER?

The general rule is that anything that is oven safe is fine for use in the air fryer, as long as it fits. Our favourites include silicone (such as pans and muffin cups), ceramic dishes (such as ramekins and casserole dishes), paper liners or metal bakeware.

Glass, such as Pyrex, is regularly used in ovens, but in the air fryer it really extends the cooking time, so we tend to avoid it.

accessories for every air fryer owner

Regardless of which air fryer model you own, we recommend that you have the following in your kitchen for your air fryer:

Spray bottle A spray bottle is essential for air frying. Simply fill an empty spray bottle with extra virgin olive oil, then use it to spray the top of your air fryer food for an extra crisp. Avoid commercial oil sprays, as they may include chemicals that cause damage to the air fryer.

Pastry brush These can be really handy for brushing egg wash onto your bread dough or pastry, or even for spreading liquid over ingredients to speed up the prep process such as spreading tomato purée over the pastry for our homemade sausage rolls (see page 202).

Thermometer Another air fryer essential is a thermometer. You can quickly check the internal temperature of meat to avoid overcooking, or just to get meat to your ideal doneness. We also use them to check cakes are baked through – insert it into the centre of the cake and if the probe comes out clean with no raw batter on it, it's done.

Non-scratch sponges When washing the air fryer you need to make sure to use non-scratch washing utensils so that you don't remove the non-stick coating. Softer, non-scratch ones avoid excessive wear and tear of the air fryer, especially if you're using an air fryer with a crisper plate and removing it to use the bottom.

Utensils As well as non-scratch sponges, we also recommend silicone utensils, such as spatulas and spoons, as these won't scratch the air fryer when you're stirring food during cooking.

Bakeware Any bakeware that fits the air fryer and would normally be used in the oven is perfect. We use round springform pans and standard cake tins in various sizes (10cm/4 inch for small air fryers or duals, or 18–20cm/7–8 inch ones for standard air fryer baskets). We also like to use mini metal trays in the air fryer oven, and the ones we have measure 24cm x 18cm/9½ x 7 inch (see page 63).

silicone is the air fryer's friend

If we could choose just one type of accessory to use, we would opt for silicone. It wipes clean or can just go in the dishwasher, making clean up effortless. For baking, you can just use silicone and avoid lining containers with baking parchment. It also comes in many different sizes, so you can always find something that fits your air fryer, and you can often use a size slightly bigger because it is bendy and you can easily adjust it to fit.

But shop around: some silicone is flimsy, so try to hunt out stronger products for your air fryer. When you buy better-quality silicone accessories, they last a long time and are better for the environment compared to single use paper liners or foil. Silicone also comes in lots of shapes and sizes, meaning no matter what size air fryer you have, you'll always find a favourite silicone that fits.

01 **Muffin cups** I use these to make our road trip muffins (see page 207) but you can also cook the sprinkle cake batter (see page 212) and make vanilla muffins with sprinkles rather than a large cake. If you are using them for muffins but want to serve them in paper liners, line the silicone cups with the paper liners and the weightier silicone will stop the paper liners from blowing around in the air fryer.

02 **Silicone cake pans** These come in many different sizes, so you will always find something to fit your air fryer. Look for sturdy silicone, as many that are marketed for the air fryer are quite flimsy. We use 9cm/3½ inch, 14cm/5½ inch and 19cm/7½ inch pans the most. We use the largest pan for cooking all our cakes in the air fryer, and for other baking recipes, such as flapjacks (see page 204). The medium size is great if you have a smaller air fryer size or are cooking a smaller portion, while the smallest pan is perfect for measuring out ingredients as well as for melting butter or chocolate in the air fryer.

03 **Round pans with handles** This is my favourite air fryer accessory of all time. It's made from sturdy silicone that lasts; I have regularly used the same pan for the last few years and it's still going strong. Thanks to the pan's handles, it's easy to move it in and out of the air fryer. It's also very deep and so it can hold a reasonable portion of food. We use it for wet foods such as chilli or our sweet potato and chickpea curry (see page 130).

04 **Dual silicone with handles** The same concept as the round pan but designed to fit the shape of dual air fryer drawers. We have two of these, so we can divide large portions of food between the two pans and cook one in each drawer, as we do for our moussaka (see page 182).

can you use ceramics in the air fryer?

Yes, you can use anything ceramic that fits in your air fryer. Ramekins are the most common ceramic to use in the air fryer. Four will normally fit a standard air fryer basket, while I can fit two in each drawer of a dual, or one to two in a smaller air fryer. Ramekins are popular because you can walk into a shop, buy them and just know that they will fit the air fryer. However, with casserole dishes you can be staring at the mini casserole dish on the shelf and wondering if you should take a chance on it! I recommend measuring the size of the inside of your air fryer at home, then subtracting 1cm/½ inch to avoid accessories being too tight a fit. Store these measurements on your phone in a notepad file, then when out shopping you're not guessing and you know the exact size limit.

01 **Ramekin dishes** Perfect for air fryers of any shape or size. We love them for little portions of our favourite recipes; see them being used in the seafood crumbles (see page 120) or as a small portion option for our cheesecake (see page 210).

02 **Square baking dishes** These are ideal for air fryers that have a square shape, such as basket or single drawer air fryers. We can easily fit 18cm/7 inch square dishes in our air fryer, but if your air fryer is smaller you may need to go down in size.

03 **Small rectangular dishes** Useful for dual air fryers as they have a smaller capacity, so you can fit one in each drawer.

04 **Larger rectangular dishes** If you have an air fryer with a flex drawer, you will be able to fit much larger baking dishes in it. Measure your drawer and buy the biggest that will fit to maximise the space you have.

accessories for small basket air fryer owners

If you own a small air fryer, you can use many of the same accessories, but for some you will just need to go smaller.

For example, I will use the spray bottle, pastry brush and thermometer as usual. However only one ramekin, rather than four in a standard basket, will fit the basket – perfect for feeding one. Then I need to choose silicone, ceramics and bakeware that fits the smaller air fryer size.

The best thing to do is get the tape measure out and check the size of your air fryer for what will fit. For example, with my small air fryer, I know I can use round accessories up to 14cm/ 5½ inches. There are a lot of shopping choices for silicone and bakeware that are smaller than this size, so it's easy to get equipped for getting started with air frying.

accessories for dual air fryer owners

If you have a dual air fryer, use the same pastry brushes, bottles, etc, but choose rectangular accessories instead of square or round ones to maximise the space in the drawers. Most useful are rectangular silicone containers with handles, which make removing the containers from narrow drawers much easier.

You also use any ceramic or metal bakeware that fits the dual baskets. However, because most dual air fryer models have removable crisper plates, you can cook items with lots of liquid directly in the bottom of the drawers, so silicone (and other) containers are used a lot less.

accessories for air fryer oven owners

If you are using an air fryer oven, you can use similar accessories as those used in basket and dual air fryers. However, the advantage is that you will be able to use wider objects, such as mini oven trays, which wouldn't fit in the other models – and which we love. (They are great for cooking two different meals, if you have a fussy partner!) Do bear in mind though that if you are cooking on more than one shelf, the depth of containers should be a consideration. Turn to our introduction to the air fryer oven on page 62 for more information.

01

04

03

02

MEAL
PREP

meal prep 101

When I first heard of meal prep, I imagined doing a bumper supermarket shop, then spending huge amounts of time making freezer meals for the whole month. But I soon learnt that meal prep could be anything you wanted it to be.

You could start with prepping some simple vegetables for the next day's dinner, or make a quiche that can be reheated when you need a snack, or marinate some meat that can make a handy base for a meal on those days when your life is crazy and you're late getting dinner cooked.

Of course, you could also do a month's meals, but it's all about what makes your life easier.

For our meal prep storage, we have a chest freezer, lots of freezer bags, and large ice cube trays (see them on page 32), but any smallish freezerproof containers will work well too.

Our main meal prep routine will include an hour or so on a Sunday prepping veggies, snacks and leftovers for the freezer to avoid food waste.

my simple sunday routine

If you want to get started with your own meal prep routine, let me introduce you to my Sunday routine. The bonus is that what I am meal prepping also becomes brunch too.

I get out my mixing bowls and favourite veggie knife (please tell me I am not the only one with a favourite knife?), then get started.

01 I start by making veggie bags (see pages 26–27), using what is left from our weekly veg box delivery to avoid any food waste. I gather the vegetables from the fridge, peel and dice them, add seasoning and oil, then bag them to use for Monday to Wednesday. If we have eaten out and have more leftover vegetables than usual, these bags can be frozen and then cooked from frozen in the air fryer without a par boil. Thanks to the oil they freeze well, and you can adjust the portion sizes in the bags to suit your household.

If you are having a Sunday lunch, you can prepare the lunch vegetables at the same time. Sometimes I will prepare the next four weeks' worth of Sunday vegetables and freeze the spare bags – it makes the next few Sundays even more stress free.

02 As I prep the veggie bags, there will be plenty of peelings, usually including parsnip, carrot and potato skins. I will have a spare bowl to collect these as they are delicious when air fried and taste just like crisps/chips (see page 28). They usually become my Sunday brunch.

03 I also like to make an impossible quiche and air fry it. It can be breakfast, a quick lunch, the basis for an evening meal, or just a snack that we can quickly reheat when we are standing in front of the fridge starving. I also love the cheat's element of this quiche that makes it very quick to prepare (see page 30).

04 I check the use-by dates on fridge supplies. This is very important if you want to save money and avoid food waste. If I have meat that is close to expiring, I will label it and freeze it. Any leftover meals that are not going to get eaten within 3 days of being made, I will freeze in portions and label them ready for another busy day.

05 If I have spare soup, sauce or curry, I will spoon it into large silicone ice cube trays. I use small ones for smaller portions; for example, leftover curry paste or marinades, or the big 240ml/1 cup version. Whichever I use, I freeze them and, once frozen, push the frozen portion out of the silicone and transfer to a freezer bag so that I can grab one from the freezer when I need it.

make-ahead rainbow veggie bags

These veggie bags are prepped and then stored in the fridge or freezer, making mealtimes even easier. As they feed one, they are perfect if you live alone and don't feel like prepping for one each day after work. Alternatively, you can double the portions to feed two, or double again to feed a family of four. They cook well from the fridge or from the freezer and perfect for busy evenings.

....

SERVES **5 BAGS**
HERO **BASKET/DUAL**
PREP **15 MINUTES**
COOK TIME **15 MINUTES**
CALORIES **205 PER BAG**

....

1½ medium butternut squashes
2 medium courgettes/zucchini
1 red (bell) pepper/capsicum
1 green (bell) pepper/capsicum
1½ tbsp extra virgin olive oil
2 tsp dried parsley
Salt and black pepper

01 Peel and dice the butternut squash into 1cm/½ inch cubes and put them in a large mixing bowl. Slice the courgette into thick slices, then quarter each slice. Deseed and dice the peppers into 1cm/½ inch chunks. Add them to the bowl with the butternut squash cubes.

02 Add your olive oil and parsley, and season with salt and pepper. Mix well with your hands until the veggies are well coated with the olive oil and seasonings.

03 Divide the seasoned veggies equally between five freezer bags and store in the fridge if using within 5 days, or freeze if you will not be using them this week.

04 When ready to air fry, tip the contents of the freezer bag (defrosted, if you have frozen it, or see below) into the air fryer basket/drawer and spread out so that they cook evenly. Set the temperature to 180ºC/360ºF and cook for 15 minutes, or until the butternut squash is fork tender. Or add an extra 5 minutes if you prefer crispier veggies.

Cooking from frozen If cooking rainbow veggie bags from frozen, tip a bag from the freezer into the air fryer, spread them out and cook at 160ºC/320ºF for 15 minutes. Shake the basket/drawer and cook for another 5 minutes at 200ºC/400ºF or until crispy to your liking.

Butternut squash swaps You can swap a similar quantity of sweet potato or pumpkin for the butternut squash and use the same time and temperature.

dom's simple potatoes & carrots

One of my favourite side dishes Dom makes us for lunch is potatoes and carrots. He will empty the bottom of the fridge, gather all the potatoes and carrots we have in, cook a big batch and bag up the remainder for other days. This recipe makes three bags, each serving two people – perfect for the next three days or to freeze for later.

....

MAKES **3 BAGS**
HERO **BASKET/DUAL**
PREP **15 MINUTES**
COOK TIME **20 MINUTES**
CALORIES **470 PER BAG**

....

7 medium red potatoes
6 medium carrots
2 tbsp extra virgin olive oil
1 tbsp dried thyme
1 tsp dried rosemary
½ tsp garlic powder
Salt and black pepper

01 Scrub the potatoes then cut them into 2.5cm/1 inch chunks. Peel and dice the carrots into 2cm/¾ inch slices.

02 Put the potatoes and carrots in a bowl and add the olive oil, herbs and garlic powder. Season with salt and pepper, and mix well with your hands until the potatoes and carrots are well coated with the olive oil and seasonings.

03 Divide the potatoes and carrots equally between three freezer bags and store in the fridge if using within 5 days, or freeze if you will not be using them this week.

04 When ready to air fry, tip the contents of the freezer bag (thawed, if you have frozen it, or see below) into the air fryer basket/drawer and spread out so that they cook evenly. Set the temperature to 180ºC/360ºF and cook for 20 minutes, or until the potatoes and carrots are fork tender. Add an extra 5 minutes if you prefer a crispier texture.

Cooking from frozen If you prefer to cook your potatoes and carrots from frozen, tip a bag from the freezer into the air fryer, spread them out and cook at 160ºC/320ºF for 20 minutes. Shake the basket/drawer and cook for another 5 minutes at 200ºC/400ºF or until crispy to your liking.

crispy curried veggie peelings

These moreish veggie snacks are made by mixing leftover vegetable peelings with olive oil and seasonings, and then they are air fried until crispy. Our favourites are using leftovers from parsnips, carrots, sweet potatoes or white potatoes, but you can mix and match any root vegetable, depending on the season.

SERVES **4**
HERO **BASKET/DUAL**
PREP **10 MINUTES**
COOK TIME **10–18 MINUTES**
CALORIES **111**

Peeled skins from 6 medium
 carrots
Peeled skins from 3 medium
 parsnips
Peeled skins from 3 medium
 white potatoes
1 tbsp extra virgin olive oil
1 heaped tsp mild curry
 powder
½ tsp ground turmeric
½ tsp garam masala
Salt and black pepper

01 Peel the vegetables as you do your meal prep, with either a knife for a thicker peeling or a peeler for a skinny peeling.

02 Add the peelings, the olive oil and spices to the bowl and season with salt and pepper. Mix well with your hands until the peelings are well coated with the olive oil and the seasonings.

03 Tip the peelings into the air fryer basket/drawer and spread out so that they cook evenly. Set the temperature to 180ºC/360ºF and cook for 10 minutes for skinny peelings or 18 minutes for thick. As air fryers differ, keep a close eye on them, and shake the drawer during cooking so that they cook evenly and don't burn.

Peeling size You can use a knife for a thicker peelings or go skinny with a vegetable peeler. The ones made with a vegetable peeler (pictured) will be crisper and more like crisps/potato chips.

cheese & tomato impossible quiche

A frittata is a quiche without any pastry, whereas an impossible quiche is a quiche with a fake pastry. You add flour to the quiche filling, then as the quiche cooks the flour drops to the bottom creating the structure of a pastry crust. It's called "impossible" because when you make it for the first time, your brain is saying "that is impossible"!

SERVES **6**
HERO **BASKET**
PREP **8 MINUTES**
COOK TIME **30 MINUTES**
CALORIES **220**

5 large eggs
120ml/4fl oz/½ cup whole/full-fat milk
2 spring onions/scallions
7 cherry tomatoes
85g/3oz/1 cup grated Cheddar cheese
2 tsp dried mixed herbs/Italian seasoning
2 tsp dried oregano
125g/4½oz/1 cup self-raising/rising-flour
Salt and black pepper

01 Crack the eggs into a mixing jug, pour in the milk and mix with a fork until combined.

02 Chop the spring onions into small chunks and halve the tomatoes. Add the spring onions, tomatoes, grated cheese and dried herbs to the jug, season with salt and pepper and mix well. Stir in the flour and mix again, making sure no flour is stuck at the bottom or down the sides.

03 Pour the mixture into a 20cm/8 inch loose-based pie tin – or a similar size that fits your air fryer. (We divide the mixture between two 10cm/4 inch pie tins in the dual air fryer). Carefully, as it will be full, transfer it to the air fryer.

04 Set the temperature to 180ºC/360ºF and cook for 20 minutes, then decrease the temperature to 160ºC/320ºF, cover with foil to avoid overbrowning on top, and cook for a further 10 minutes, or until a thermometer probe comes out clean. Allow it to sit in the air fryer basket to cool a little as the air fryer cools down, as then it's easier to remove from the air fryer. Serve the quiche warm or cold, though in the Milner house we like it cold and to take with us for picnic food.

You must try quiche bites! Sometimes leftovers taste better than the original recipe and this is one of those times. Chop leftover quiche into squares, then place into the air fryer. Air fry at 200ºC/400ºF for 4 minutes and you have something that can only be described as croutons meets flavoured bread. So good!

bits & bobs freezer sauce for everything

My favourite way to make a sauce is to gather up different veggies that need using up, to avoid wastage. I cook them until tender, then blend and use as base for a sauce that can be transformed into different sauces depending on what meals we are eating. We will then freeze in 240ml/ 1 cup portions which can be used when needed.

MAKES **4 FREEZER CUBES**
HERO **DUAL**
PREP **15 MINUTES**
COOK TIME **40 MINUTES**
CALORIES **373 PER CUBE**

6 medium tomatoes
3 medium carrots
1 medium courgette/zucchini
225g/8oz butternut squash, peeled and deseeded
1 tbsp extra virgin olive oil
1 tbsp dried parsley
1 garlic bulb
1 × 150g/5½oz pack garlic and herb cream cheese (we use Boursin)
2 tsp dried basil
240ml/8fl oz/1 cup whole milk/full-fat milk, plus extra if needed
Salt and black pepper

01 Quarter the tomatoes and peel and slice the carrots. Slice the courgette into 1cm/½ inch slices and then into quarters. Peel the butternut squash and chop it into 2cm/¾ inch cubes. Put all the vegetables in the air fryer drawer, removing the crisper plate first. Add the olive oil and parsley, and season generously with salt and pepper. Mix well with your hands until the vegetables are well coated with the oil and seasonings.

02 Slice the top off the garlic bulb exposing the cloves at the top. Spray with olive oil and season with salt and pepper. Wrap tightly in foil and place in the air fryer on top of the vegetables. Set the temperature to 180°C/360°F and cook for 30 minutes.

03 Remove the foil-wrapped garlic and shake the air fryer drawer to rotate the vegetables. Unwrap the cream cheese and place over the vegetables. Sprinkle half the basil over the cheese and air fry at the same temperature for a further 10 minutes.

04 Meanwhile, pour the milk into a blender or food processor. Squeeze the soft flesh out of the garlic head, discarding the papery skin, and add it to the blender. When the air fryer beeps, tip the contents of the air fryer drawer into the blender – including any juices that have collected – and add the remaining basil. Pulse until you have a creamy sauce, adding a little extra milk if it's too thick.

05 If freezing, pour the sauce into large 240ml/1 cup freezer cubes (or into small freezer-proof boxes) and allow to cool before adding the lid and freezing.

Basket sauce Combine the ingredients in a mixing bowl, then divide it between two silicone containers that fit your air fryer (ours are 20cm/8 inch) and cook one at a time, following the same time and temperature as mentioned above. I will usually do the garlic bulb in one batch and the cheese in the other.

Bits and bobs You can mix and match vegetables you have in, but try to balance naturally starchy vegetables, such as root vegetables, with vegetables with a higher water content, such as tomatoes or courgette. If you just add watery vegetables, your sauce will be too thin, and with too many root vegetables, it will be too thick.

Sauce suggestions Use the sauce as your base for:
Cheese sauce – add 225g/8oz/2½ cups grated Cheddar cheese.
Tomato sauce – swap the milk for a 400g/14oz passata.
Mexican sauce – swap the milk for 400g/14oz of salsa.

let's chop up a chicken

We first started jointing chickens when we moved into an apartment in Portugal. It was 2009 and whole chickens were often on clearance and much cheaper than buying different parts of the chicken – and perfect for buying in bulk. It gave us a choice. We could chop the legs, we could have skin-on chicken breasts, or we could collect chicken wings in a freezer bag and freeze ready for game night.

First, we're going to show you how to chop up a chicken, then we'll share with you the marinades we use with our pieces of chicken, and provide cooking times and temperatures for the different cuts. If marinated chicken is not your thing, you can freeze the chicken as it is in freezer bags, then thaw and air fry following the same cooking instructions (see page 37).

01 Place your whole chicken on a chopping board and grab your favourite sharp knife. Use one hand to hold a leg slightly away from the breast and cut through the skin at the joint. Pull the leg away from the bird and you should be able to see the joint. Cut through it to remove the leg, then repeat to remove the other leg.

02 To divide the leg into thigh and drumstick, place the leg on the board and feel for the joint. Slice the skin there so that you can see it, then take one end of the leg in each hand and bend the leg backwards until you feel it pop out. Get your knife into the loosened joint and cut down firmly to separate the pieces, then do the same again for the other chicken leg.

03 Feel for the backbone of the chicken and cut down the side of it to remove the breast. Keep your knife as close to the bone as you can as you cut the breast from the carcass so that you don't waste any chicken. Then slice all the way down to the bottom, removing the wing with the breast. Repeat to remove the other breast and wing. This is called a "supreme" and you can use it like this, but we like to remove the wings and cook those separately.

04 To remove the wing from the breast, carefully cut around the joint at the base of the breast. You will now have eight chicken pieces.

You have now chopped up a chicken: congratulations!

We now recommend deciding on what you plan to cook straight away and what you plan to freeze – and how to incorporate your various chicken pieces into your meal prep routine.

We usually chop up about four whole chickens at once so that we have plenty for our meal prep routine. We will prepare bags of just drumsticks; mixed drumsticks and thighs; full legs; and skin-on chicken breasts.

Also consider how many portions you would like to thaw and cook together. For example, cooking for our family will normally require four chicken leg portions, so we will freeze four of them together in a single heavy-duty freezer bag.

To avoid dinner boredom and not feel like you're cooking the same food everyday, you'll find our flavourful go-to marinades on the next page.

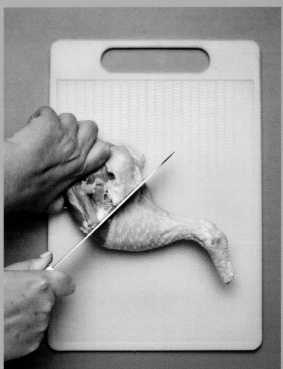

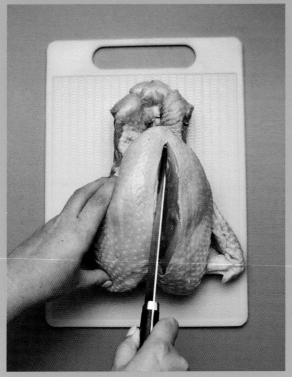

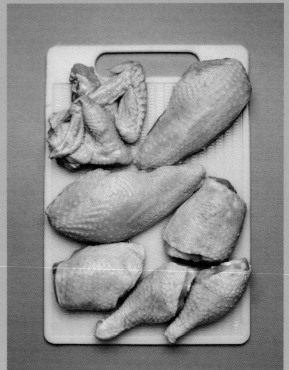

7 marinades for everything

After a long day at work, there is nothing more satisfying than grabbing a bag of marinated chicken breasts from the fridge (or freezer), placing them straight in the air fryer and putting your feet up. These seven marinades were originally created for chicken, but we also use them regularly with pork chops, fish fillets and tofu.

marinate in 5 simple steps

01 Choose your container Think of what you're using in the air fryer. If that's a foil tray/pan then choose this, or if you are air frying directly in the basket/drawer or want to save freezer space then opt for freezer bags. Though make sure that the freezer bags you use are the heavy duty ones that can handle the marinade.

02 Choose your protein We find the marinade ingredients are perfect for 750g/1lb 10oz of protein such as: 4 chicken legs, 6 chicken thighs, 8 chicken drumsticks, 8 chicken wings, 4 chicken breasts, 4 pork chops, 8 salmon fillets or 450g/1lb pressed (see page 145) tofu.

03 Choose your marinade We like to mix it up and do a variety of marinades to make mealtime more fun. Choose your favourite, or do a variety.

04 Prepare everything Set up a batch system and make the marinades first in the storage containers, then batch add the proteins and give them a good mix.

05 Fridge vs freezer If you plan to consume your marinated protein within 3 days, store in the fridge and allow to marinate for at least 2 hours before air frying. Or label and freeze for up to 3 months. Check out the tip on page 38 for how to cook from frozen.

Top tips

You don't have to batch You could use this page as your guide and simply marinate some chicken breasts for dinner.

Prepare in containers Use the container as your mixing bowl and save on washing up. You could prepare in a foil tray, freeze, thaw and air fry all in the same tray.

Reserve a little If making for tonight, you can also reserve a little marinade (1 tablespoon is a good amount) to brush over your protein just before serving. (Make sure you put it in a different bowl and don't use the marinade from the raw meat.)

Serving Once cooked, you can use your marinated chicken protein in a salad, serve with one of our vegetable recipes, or have it for sandwiches – the choice is yours. But do look out for these marinades in action throughout the book.

Paper liners We love using paper liners for marinated foods. As you can cook the food on the paper liner, you don't have a messy air fryer to deal with, and you can transfer your food from the freezer bag directly to the paper liner.

Pat's pans We love that Pat, an air fryer oven user of many years, streamlines her cooking by using foil trays/pans instead of cooking directly in the air fryer. The marinade can be mixed up in the trays, so the food can be prepped, frozen and cooked all in the same container, and then discarded after use to save on washing up too! You can do the same with the basket, or drawer air fryers – just find a pan that fits.

CORIANDER/CILANTRO LIME

2 tbsp lime juice
3 tbsp extra virgin olive oil
2 tbsp clear honey
1 tsp garlic purée
2 tbsp finely chopped fresh coriander/cilantro
Salt and black pepper

CURRY YOGHURT

1 tsp garlic purée
1 tsp ginger purée
1 tbsp extra virgin olive oil
3 tbsp Greek yoghurt
2 tsp mild curry powder
1 tsp ground turmeric
1 tsp ground cumin
1 tsp dried coriander/cilantro leaf
Salt and black pepper

GREEK KEBABS

2 tsp garlic purée
1 tbsp balsamic vinegar
1 tbsp lemon juice
1 tbsp extra virgin olive oil
2 tbsp Greek yoghurt
2 tsp dried oregano
Salt and black pepper

HAWAIIAN SUMMER

2 tbsp pineapple juice
2 tbsp barbecue sauce
1 tbsp tomato ketchup
Juice and finely grated zest of 1 lime
1 tbsp extra virgin olive oil
1 tsp garlic purée
1 tsp ginger purée
1 tsp ground cumin
1 tsp smoked paprika
Salt and black pepper

HONEY & GARLIC

1 tbsp white wine vinegar
1 tbsp extra virgin olive oil
2 tsp garlic purée
100g/3½oz/⅓ cup clear honey
¼ tsp dried parsley
Salt and black pepper

MOROCCAN SPICE

1 tsp garlic purée
1 tsp ginger purée

2 tsp tomato purée/paste
1 tsp harissa paste
4 tbsp passata
2 tbsp extra virgin olive oil
1 tsp dried coriander/cilantro leaf
1 tsp ground cumin
1 tsp smoked paprika
¼ tsp ground cinnamon
Salt and black pepper

SWEET CHILLI

240g/8½oz/¾ cup sweet chilli sauce
1 tsp garlic purée
1 tsp ginger purée
2 tsp soy sauce
¼ red (bell) pepper/capsicum, finely chopped
½ tsp Chinese 5-spice powder
Salt and black pepper

01 Choose a marinade from the list. Add the marinade ingredients to a heavy-duty freezer bag or mix them up in a foil tray/pan.

02 Add the meat, fish or tofu to the bag and mix well with your hands.

03 Transfer the container to the fridge or freezer. If you are planning on cooking it that day, allow to marinate for at least 2 hours beforehand.

04 Transfer the protein to the air fryer basket/drawer, placing it either on a paper liner or keeping it in its foil container. Set the temperature to 180°C/360°F, then follow the relevant cook time below:

Chicken drumsticks – 17 minutes
Chicken thighs – 23 minutes
Chicken legs – 25 minutes
Small (140g/5oz) chicken breasts – 15 minutes
Medium (200g/7oz) chicken breasts – 20 minutes
Large (250g/9oz) chicken breasts – 25 minutes
Frozen chicken wings – 20 minutes
Pork chops – 18 minutes
Salmon fillets – 12 minutes
Tofu cubes – 12 minutes

marinated chicken snack bags

You're probably wondering what to do with marinated chicken; well, picture yourself standing in front of the fridge, wishing you had something easy to eat right now. These snack bags are full of thinly sliced marinated chicken that you can grab as you need it – it can become a sandwich, be used in salads, snack on when starving, or take with you on long walks or road trips. You can also mix and match with any of our marinades.

....

SERVES **4**
HERO **BASKET/DUAL**
PREP **2 MINUTES**
COOK TIME **20 MINUTES**
CALORIES **138 (WITHOUT MARINADE)**

....

4 medium chicken breasts in marinade (see pages 36–7), thawed
Salt and black pepper

01 Remove the chicken breasts from the freezer bag that you marinated them in and place onto a paper liner inside your air fryer basket/drawer. Pour over any remaining marinade left in the freezer bag.

02 Set the temperature to 180ºC/360ºF and cook for 20 minutes, or until the chicken breasts have reached an internal temperature of 70ºC/160ºF or above.

03 Let the chicken rest for a couple of minutes, then season with salt and pepper and cut into thin slices. Once cold, transfer to food bags and store in the fridge for snack time – they will last 2–3 days.

Freezer friendly snacking You can also store your just-cooked chicken in snack bags in the freezer. Once cool, transfer the chicken snack slices to an oven tray, then freeze for an hour on the tray to firm up. Transfer the slices to freezer bags, seal and freeze for up to 3 months. Because you have pre-frozen them spread out on the tray, the chicken slices won't stick to each other once bagged up. If you don't want to wait for them to thaw, place the slices of frozen chicken into the air fryer basket/drawer and air fry at 150ºC/300ºF for 10 minutes to defrost.

Cooking from frozen Raw chicken breasts that have been frozen in their marinade are so moist and flavourful. Simply remove them from the freezer bag and place onto a paper liner inside your air fryer basket/drawer. Alternatively, if you have frozen them in a foil tray, remove the lid from your foil tray and place the tray in the air fryer. Cook at 120ºC/250ºF for 18 minutes to defrost the chicken. Turn the chicken over with tongs and increase the temperature to 160ºC/320ºF. Cook for a further 14 minutes or until the chicken breasts have reached an internal temperature of 70ºC/160ºF or above.

BBQ shredded chicken wraps

Our favourite thing about cooking a rotisserie chicken (see page 73) is that air fryer chicken is a lot moister than oven-roasted chicken. Shredding the leftover chicken and enjoying a day or two later is amazing. After a few add-ins, you have delicious barbecue chicken wraps that are freezer friendly too.

....

MAKES **4**
HERO **BASKET/DUAL**
PREP **5 MINUTES**
COOK TIME **8 MINUTES**
CALORIES **367**

....

240g/8½oz/1½ cups shredded chicken from rotisserie chicken (see page 73)
120g/4¼oz/½ cup barbecue sauce
70g/2½oz/½ cup canned sweetcorn, drained
85g/3oz/1 cup grated mozzarella cheese
1 tbsp dried basil
4 mini tortilla wraps
4 tsp cream cheese
1 egg, beaten for egg wash
Salt and black pepper

01 In a mixing bowl, combine the leftover shredded rotisserie chicken, barbecue sauce, sweetcorn, grated cheese and basil. Season generously with salt and pepper, and mix with your hands until the chicken is well coated.

02 Using a butter knife, spread a wrap with a layer of cream cheese, then add 3 heaped tablespoons of the barbecue chicken. Roll up the wrap tightly, tucking the sides in as you go, to stop it coming apart, then brush the top of the wrap with egg wash. Repeat to fill and roll all the wraps.

03 Place the wraps into the air fryer basket/drawer. In our basket air fryer, we can fit four wraps in at once, while in the dual we can fit three in each drawer; do it in batches if you need to.

04 Set the temperature to 180ºC/360ºF and cook for 6 minutes. Flip the wraps over and egg wash the other sides, then cook for a final 2 minutes. Serve warm.

Wraps for the freezer The BBQ chicken wraps above are perfect for easy meal prep and for using up leftovers. You can also prep the wraps, but instead of air frying straight away, wrap them in foil and place in the freezer. Defrost when you want one and cook following the instructions above.

PANTRY

pantry ingredients

When I was 16 and had fallen on hard times, I met a lovely lady and she let me sleep on her sofa. She was on a low income and did a lot of cooking from pantry staples. She bulk bought canned and other pantry foods and would top each up to a quantity of six. Then, if she went a week without being able to afford groceries, this was her back up. Even now, almost 25 years later, I still stack my pantry in volumes of six. With the cost of living crisis, pantry foods, which can taste delicious, have made a comeback and have become very popular for cooking in the air fryer.

canned goods cooking times

Thoroughly drain your listed canned veggies and pat dry with kitchen paper. Put them in a bowl with 2 teaspoons of extra virgin olive oil and 1 teaspoon of your favourite dried seasonings. Mix well with your hands and load into the air fryer.

Whole mushrooms 180°C/360°F – 8 minutes

Mixed vegetables 180°C/360°F – 15 minutes

Baby potatoes 180°C/360°F – 20 minutes

Whole baby carrots 180°C/360°F – 20 minutes

Sliced baby carrots 180°C/360°F – 15 minutes

Peas 180°C/360°F – 6 minutes

Sweetcorn 180°C/360°F – 6 minutes

7 pantry ingredients we always have in

Canned tomatoes and/or passata Chopped tomatoes are fantastic for making sauces, and you can blend them if you prefer a smooth sauce. Or if you prefer smooth sauces without any blending, swap canned tomatoes for passata.

Canned tuna I always buy it in brine rather than oil. It's perfect for a last minute tuna melt or a salad.

Canned sweetcorn The can of many uses: tuna melts, salads, air fried into a crispy snack, or use it for bulking up recipes to feed more mouths.

Canned chickpeas If I have a favourite meal in the air fryer it is my sweet potato and chickpea curry (see page 130). Chickpeas, like sweetcorn, are also ideal for salads, snacking on and bulking up meals.

Canned taco beans mix I love these cans of Mexican deliciousness. Instead of mixing up lots of different cans, these combinations of various types of bean in a spicy tomato sauce are a fantastic add in. We use them in quesadillas (see page 52), or in place of the red kidney beans in a chilli con carne (see page 55).

Canned brown lentils Forget dried lentils, with the air fryer cans of brown lentils are a fast solution. Try them toasted (page 58).

Canned whole potatoes These have become a very popular pantry staple for the air fryer and OMG these are delicious and now a Milner mealtime favourite.

Because we like to practise what we preach, you will find all these canned ingredients used throughout the book.

other supplies you will always find in our pantry

- Coconut milk
- Pineapple
- Beans: black, black-eyed, baked
- Extra virgin olive oil
- Balsamic vinegar
- Worcestershire sauce
- Honey
- Maple syrup
- Wholegrain mustard
- Tomato purée/paste
- Garlic purée
- Ginger purée
- Cocoa powder
- Sugar: icing/confectioner's, light brown, granulated
- Flour: self-raising/self-rising, plain/all-purpose

10 herbs and spices we use the most

We much prefer to use dried herbs and spices because they are easy to store, making everyday cooking so much easier. They also travel well, so we pack them to add instant flavour to our holiday meals. Below are the ones we use the most at home (and therefore in these recipes), along with salt and pepper:

- Mixed herbs/Italian seasoning
- Oregano
- Basil
- Thyme
- Rosemary
- Mint
- Dill
- Smoked paprika or sweet paprika
- Mixed spice or pumpkin spice
- Cumin

brilliant breadcrumbs

Homemade breadcrumbs don't cook as well as shop-bought crumbs in the air fryer. They struggle to crisp up and can look pale. Instead, choose from these three pantry staples:

Panko breadcrumbs These will give you the crisp on your food that in texture will be very similar to breaded food you normally eat, and a good golden colour.

Golden breadcrumbs These are popular in the UK and have a deep golden colour, reminiscent to that on fish fingers/fish sticks.

Shake 'N Bake These are the US favourite. You can get them in different flavours, which means they are useful for mixing and matching flavours depending on what you are coating.

how to start your own pantry

If you have never stocked a pantry before, you can start slow, check out special deals and build it up over time.

We notice, when shopping, that the best deals will be in your eyeline so that the shop can bring them to your attention – or they might also be on prominent end-of-aisle displays. Pantry staples are often on 'buy one get one free' deals so you can stock up whenever items are on offer. Soon you will have a pantry stocked for easy everyday recipes.

20-minute herby canned potatoes

I hadn't eaten a canned potato in more than 20 years, yet here I was, trying them in the air fryer after a reader asked for them. I was pleasantly surprised by how delicious this simple staple tasted and now I have a pantry stocked with canned potatoes!

....

SERVES **2**
HERO **BASKET/DUAL**
PREP **8 MINUTES**
COOK TIME **20 MINUTES**
CALORIES **176**

....

1 × 540g/19oz can potatoes
½ tbsp extra virgin olive oil
½ tsp dried parsley
A pinch of dried rosemary
A pinch of garlic powder
Extra virgin olive oil spray
Salt and black pepper

01 Drain the potatoes, then gently place them onto a piece of kitchen paper/paper towel. Let the potatoes sit for 5 minutes to soak up the extra moisture.

02 Very gently place the potatoes into a bowl; try not to be heavy-handed as the potatoes are pre-cooked and preserved in water and can break easily. Add the olive oil, herbs and garlic powder and season with salt and pepper. Mix with your hands until the potatoes are well coated.

03 Tip the potatoes into the air fryer basket/drawer and spread them out. Set the temperature to 180ºC/360ºF and cook for 15 minutes. When the air fryer beeps, the potatoes will be almost golden. To create a crisper texture, spray the potatoes with olive oil, increase the temperature to 200ºC/400ºF and air fry for an extra 5 minutes before serving.

Slices are even better Whilst I love whole canned potatoes, cutting each baby potato into slices really adds a wow factor – the crisp is better and it's like a crunchy feast. Follow the technique above, but after patting dry, slice each potato into 5mm/¼ inch slices. Add the same amount of oil and seasonings and air fry the sliced potatoes for the same time and temperature as above. We use these in our Monday pie recipe (see page 180).

Add canned baby carrots We love that canned potatoes and baby carrots carry the same cook time. Simply follow the baby potatoes recipe, but also drain and pat dry a **300g/10½oz can of baby carrots**. Add 50 per cent more of the oil and seasonings to the bowl to give the carrots and potatoes a great taste, and continue with the recipe as above.

dom's stuffed tuna melts

If there is one pantry staple we always have in, its canned tuna. Dom makes tuna melts in the air fryer from his favourite shop-bought cheesy bread, filled with onion, sweetcorn, mayo and plenty of cheese. They're so delicious.

SERVES **4**
HERO **BASKET/DUAL**
PREP **8 MINUTES**
COOK TIME **8 MINUTES**
CALORIES **699**

2 × 145g/5oz cans tuna in brine
1 × 160g/5½oz can sweetcorn
¼ medium red onion, peeled
 and finely diced
1 tbsp cream cheese
5 tbsp mayonnaise
½ tsp wholegrain mustard
1 tsp dried parsley
1 tsp dried oregano
115g/4oz/1¼ cups grated
 mature/sharp Cheddar
 cheese
2 cheese cob loaves or
 4 individual rolls
Salt and black pepper

01 Drain the tuna and sweetcorn and tip them both into a mixing bowl. To the bowl, add the onion, cream cheese, mayonnaise, mustard, parsley, oregano and three-quarters of the Cheddar. Season with salt and pepper, mix well, then set aside.

02 Next, use a serrated knife to cut the crust off the top of the bread. Cut out the fluffy insides of the bread, going just halfway down the loaf so that there is a hollow at the top, but a thick layer of bread at the base to create a bread boat. Add one-quarter of the removed bread pieces to the tuna bowl.

03 Mix the bread chunks into the tuna mixture before using a spoon to distribute the filling between the two bread boats. Press down to fit more into each bread cob. Sprinkle with the remaining Cheddar on top and press the cheese down to stop it escaping when being air fried.

04 Place the tuna melts into the air fryer basket, or place one in each drawer. Set the temperature to 180ºC/360ºF and cook for 8 minutes. When the air fryer beeps the cheese will be melted and golden and the bread will be starting to get crispy.

corned beef hash

I love corned beef hash and it takes me back to my childhood. My Grandma would always talk about how corned beef was the hero ingredient during Second World War rationing and how the local soldiers would give her their corned beef ration to feed her young daughters. Corned beef hash is one of those old-fashioned greats that is just perfect cooked in the air fryer.

SERVES **2**
HERO **BASKET/DUAL**
PREP **8 MINUTES**
COOK TIME **36 MINUTES**
CALORIES **857**

4 medium white potatoes
2 large carrots
2 tsp mixed herbs/Italian
  seasoning
1 tbsp extra virgin olive oil
1 small onion
1 × 340g/11¾oz can corned
  beef
Salt and black pepper
1 × 400g/14oz can baked
  beans, to serve (optional)

01 Scrub the potatoes, then dice them into 1cm/½in cubes. Peel and dice the carrots into a cubes of a similar size. Put the potatoes, carrots, mixed herbs and olive oil in a bowl, season with salt and pepper, and mix well with your hands.

02 Tip the potato and carrot mixture into the air fryer basket/drawer and spread out for an even cook. Set the temperature to 180ºC/360ºF and cook for 20 minutes.

03 Meanwhile, peel and finely slice the onion and, when the air fryer beeps, add it to the air fryer. Shake the basket/drawer to combine everything, then air fry at the same temperature for a further 8 minutes.

04 Whilst the potatoes, carrots and onion are cooking, open a can of corned beef and cut it into 2cm/¾ inch chunks. When the air fryer beeps, shake the air fryer and add the corned beef chunks on top. If you are serving your corned beef hash with baked beans, divide them between two ramekins. Find a space in the air fryer for the ramekins.

05 Cook the hash and the beans for 8 minutes until the corned beef is crisping up and the beans are heated through, then serve your corned beef hash with the beans.

taco bean & cheese quesadillas

If I close my eyes and enjoy a quick daydream, I am back in Mexico eating the most delicious quesadillas. If you are having a pantry clear out, that can of taco beans and those wraps you forgot about are ideal for a quick taste of Mexico.

....

SERVES **2**
HERO **BASKET**
PREP **8 MINUTES**
COOK TIME **8 MINUTES**
CALORIES **893**

....

4 small tortilla wraps
2 tbsp sour cream
3 tbsp extra virgin olive oil
1 tsp frozen chopped garlic
1 tsp dried coriander/cilantro
  leaf
1 × 400g/14oz can mixed taco
  beans in tomato sauce
1 spring onion/scallion, finely
  sliced
1 tsp taco seasoning
4 tbsp salsa
85g/3oz/1 cup grated
  Cheddar cheese
Salt and black pepper

01 Place the four mini wraps on a worktop and spread sour cream over two of them, spreading it close to the edge, as it will work like egg wash for keeping the wraps in place as they air fry.

02 Mix together the olive oil, garlic and coriander in a bowl, then brush it over the tops of the other two wraps.

03 Drain the can of taco beans and tip the beans into a mixing bowl; reserve the tomato sauce in a separate dish. Add the spring onion, taco seasoning and 1 tablespoon of the salsa to the beans, and mix well. Season with salt and pepper, then spoon the bean mixture over the sour cream coated wraps. Sprinkle over the grated cheese and top with the other wraps, oil side up, and press down to seal.

04 Gently place a quesadilla into the air fryer basket, set the temperature to 180ºC/360ºF and cook for 8 minutes, or until the tortilla is crispy and the cheese has melted. Repeat to cook the second quesadilla, if necessary.

05 While the quesadillas are air frying, mix the reserved sauce from the beans with the remaining salsa. When the air fryer beeps, serve the quesadillas with the salsa dip.

Dual quesadillas To make quesadillas that fit into the dual drawers, we use half the amount of filling in one wrap, spreading it over one half of the tortilla, then fold the tortilla over to make a semi-circular quesadilla, like you would a pasty. You can use the same time and temperature and put one folded quesadilla in each drawer. Then when it's time to serve, slice them in half instead of into quarters.

cook-once eat-twice chilli con carne

Known in the UK as 'chilli con carne' and in the USA simply as 'chili', this is a delicious dish when cooked in the air fryer. It can be stretched to feed more mouths thanks to the pantry staples that bulk up this famous one pot dinner. Serve with quesadillas for the ultimate pantry dinner, or why not load up the chilli con carne over some homemade flatbread from page 196.

....

SERVES **4**

HERO **DUAL**

PREP **5 MINUTES**

COOK TIME **39 MINUTES**

CALORIES **443**

....

450g/1lb minced beef/ground beef

1 medium carrot, peeled and finely diced

1 medium white onion, diced

1 × 500g/1lb 2oz jar chilli sauce

1 × 400g/14oz can kidney beans, drained

1 × 400g/14oz can chopped tomatoes

1 tbsp mixed herbs/Italian seasoning

1 heaped tsp cayenne pepper, or to taste

2 tsp smoked paprika

Salt and black pepper

01 Remove the crisper plate from your dual air fryer and place the minced beef directly into the bottom of the air fryer, or into a silicone dish if using an air fryer basket. Sprinkle the carrot and onion over the mince.

02 Set the temperature to 180ºC/360ºF and cook for 5 minutes, then use a wooden spoon to break up the mince. Cook for another 4 minutes.

03 When the air fryer beeps, add the remaining ingredients, season with salt and pepper, and mix well. If you like a spicier chilli, increase the cayenne pepper to suit your taste buds.

04 Air fry the chilli for a further 30 minutes at the same temperature, or until the chilli is piping hot throughout. We recommend a quick stir halfway through the cooking time to prevent the kidney beans becoming overly crispy on top.

Leftover-chilli dogs Chilli dogs (in photo, left) are perfect for using up a little leftover chilli – and, made in the air fryer with melted cheese, even better. Simply cook **4 frankfurters/large hotdogs** at 180ºC/360ºF for 8 minutes, until cooked through. Load them into **4 hotdog buns**, then spoon **leftover chilli** over each one. Top each with **a sprinkling of Cheddar cheese** and load them back into the air fryer. Cook at the same temperature for another 8 minutes to heat the chilli and melt the cheese, before serving. Sprinkle with **sliced fresh chilli** and **spring onions/scallions** to serve, if you like.

hawaiian chicken salad

SERVES **4**
HERO **BASKET/DUAL**
PREP **15 MINUTES, PLUS MARINATING**
COOK TIME **23 MINUTES**
CALORIES **499**

4 medium chicken breasts
1 recipe quantity Hawaiian
  Summer Marinade
  (see page 37)

FOR THE CHICKEN BREADING
45g/1½oz/1 cup panko
  breadcrumbs
20g/¾oz/¼ cup desiccated/
  dried shredded coconut
2 tsp smoked paprika
A pinch of garlic powder

FOR THE SALAD
1 little gem lettuce
¼ red onion
8 cherry tomatoes
1 medium avocado
1 red (bell) pepper/capsicum
4 slices canned pineapple
  (in juice)
70g/2½oz/½ cup drained
  canned sweetcorn

FOR THE DRESSING
2 tbsp extra virgin olive oil
3 tbsp pineapple juice (from
  the can of sliced pineapple)
½ tsp garlic purée
½ tsp ginger purée
2 tbsp maple syrup
A squeeze of lime juice
A pinch of smoked paprika
Salt and black pepper

This Hawaiian chicken salad is my summer clear-out recipe, with lots of bits and bobs going in: spare salad items, marinated chicken from the freezer, along with lots of favourite canned staples. This is brilliant for your next barbecue.

01 Put the chicken and the marinade in a bowl and mix well with your hands, then cover with cling film/plastic wrap. Leave to marinate in the fridge for at least 2 hours, or you can leave it overnight if you prefer.

02 When ready to cook, combine the breading ingredients on a large plate and mix well. Roll each marinated chicken breast in the breading until well coated, shaking to remove any excess.

03 Place the chicken breasts in the air fryer basket, spreading them out; if using the dual air fryer, place two breasts in each drawer. Set the temperature to 180°C/360°F and cook for 15 minutes. When the air fryer beeps, increase the temperature to 200°C/400°F and air fry for a further 8 minutes, or until the chicken reaches an internal temperature of 70°C/160°F or above.

04 Whilst the chicken is cooking, prepare the salad. Wash and shred the lettuce, peel and slice the red onion and slice the cherry tomatoes in half. Stone and peel, then slice the avocado, and deseed and dice the red pepper. Slice the pineapple into chunks, then drain the canned sweetcorn. Layer up your salad on a serving plate, starting with the lettuce, then set aside.

05 When the air fryer beeps, remove the chicken from the air fryer and place on a chopping board. While it rests, combine your salad dressing ingredients in a jug, season with salt and pepper, and mix with a fork.

06 Slice the chicken and add to the salad, then finish with a drizzle of your salad dressing.

toasted lentils

I love draining cans of pantry staples, such as chickpeas and sweetcorn, then making them crispy and yummy in the air fryer. Toasted lentils are my new favourite. They are perfect for sprinkling on salads or soups, or make a guilt-free evening snack.

....

SERVES **4**
HERO **DUAL/BASKET**
PREP **5 MINUTES**
COOK TIME **8 MINUTES**
CALORIES **101**

....

1 × 400g/14oz can brown
  lentils
1 tbsp extra virgin olive oil
1 tbsp dried oregano
Salt and black pepper

01 Thoroughly drain the can of lentils, then tip them onto a couple of pieces of kitchen towel/paper towel to dry them further and soak up all the excess moisture.

02 Transfer the lentils to a bowl and add the olive oil and oregano, along with a generous seasoning of salt and pepper. Mix well with your hands.

03 Tip the lentils into the air fryer basket/drawer and spread out. If using an air fryer with a crisper plate, remove the plate and cook them directly in the bottom. Set the temperature to 200ºC/400ºF and cook for 8 minutes, or until crispy to your liking.

Waste not If using a basket, some of the toasted lentils may have escaped the basket into the bottom of the air fryer. Simply remove the basket and tip these extra-crispy lentils into your serving bowl with the others – they will also be delicious.

Mix up the flavours If oregano is not your thing, swap the 1 tablespoon of oregano for the same quantity of curry powder, taco seasoning, Southern Fried seasoning, piri piri or Cajun spice mix. Or try ½ tablespoon each of dried parsley and dill together, or team up smoked paprika and ground cumin.

Crispy cumin chickpeas Try switching the lentils for a can of chickpeas and swapping the oregano for cumin to make crispy cumin chickpeas. We use these on top of hummus for our mezze (see page 185).

crispy dill pickle chips

I have lost count of the times I have ordered a quarter pounder at a fast-food chain and asked for extra gherkins/pickles. But it wasn't until I first visited the US that I realised there was a much better way to enjoy gherkins and that was in a delicious breading. With this crispy dill pickle chips recipe, they are so easy to re-create in your air fryer.

....

SERVES **4**
HERO **BASKET/DUAL**
PREP **10 MINUTES**
COOK TIME **8 MINUTES**
CALORIES **97**

....

1 × 340g/12oz jar sliced
  gherkins/pickles
35g/1¼oz/¼ cup plain flour/
  all-purpose flour
1 large egg
28g/1oz/½ cup panko
  breadcrumbs
1 tbsp dried dill
2 pinches of cayenne pepper
2 pinches of garlic powder
Salt and black pepper

01 Thoroughly drain the gherkins, then place them on a couple of pieces of kitchen towel/paper towel to dry them further and soak up all the excess extra moisture. Drain them again on some fresh kitchen paper, as gherkins do carry a lot of liquid.

02 Set up your production line for the breading. Put the flour in a shallow bowl. Crack the egg into another bowl, season with salt and pepper, then beat the egg with a fork and set aside. Put the breadcrumbs in a third shallow bowl, add the dill, cayenne pepper and garlic powder, season with salt and pepper, and stir with a fork. You're now ready to bread your gherkins.

03 One at a time, place the gherkins into the flour, turning to coat, then drench in the egg. Finally, roll them in the breadcrumb mixture to give them a good coating.

04 Place the gherkin chips in the air fryer basket/drawer and spread out. If you're using a dual air fryer you can spread them out over two drawers. Set the temperature to 200°C/400°F and cook for 6 minutes, then turn them over and cook for a further 2 minutes until golden and crispy to your liking.

Reserve the pickle juices Those juices from a jar of gherkins are amazing for using in sauces or marinades. Our favourite is in the burger sauce on page 108, as part of our burger in a bowl.

AIR FRYER OVEN

getting to know your air fryer oven

WHAT IS AN AIR FRYER OVEN?

Air fryer ovens use the same cooking technology as the basket or drawer models, but are more similar in appearance to a standard oven, although much smaller in size. Like an oven, they come with shelves which slot into grooves at the sides, although in an air fryer oven you can cook food directly on the shelves.

The main benefit of air fryer ovens is their size. They are usually about 10 litres – giving them twice the capacity of standard basket models. This means that you can cook the same amount of food as in two air fryer baskets or the same as in one dual. You are also not as restricted in accessory size as there is more space on the shelves to use mini oven trays, for example, which wouldn't be possible in other models.

Another huge bonus of air fryer ovens is the rotisserie that comes with most models, which is brilliant for rotating your favourite roasting meats, as well as for kebabs. I can never decide between gyros (see page 77) or Brazilian barbecue (see page 70) for the best thing to make with it.

There are some benefits of standard air fryers which the oven models miss out on. Firstly, if you are buying an air fryer to save on energy bills, it's not as good an option. Because it's like a mini oven, we find it costs a lot more to run compared to other air fryers we own.

Additionally, as they are much bigger than standard air fryers, they don't heat up as quickly and so will need preheating. (We recommend a preheat of 2 minutes before adding your food.) Food also does not cook as quickly in the oven models as it does in basket or drawer models.

The air fryer oven is best for people who prefer traybakes, or who are looking for a smaller version of the oven. It's also great for those who love entertaining, as the rotisserie is an appealing function for wowing your friends. They are also good if you want a larger air fryer to cook a greater volume of food.

air fryer oven shelves

In air fryer communities, "rack" is the name often given to the shelves in an air fryer oven, because they look similar to cooling racks. They are also sometimes numbered in air fryer recipes, so the top shelf would be "shelf one", the next down "shelf two" and so on.

But not all air fryer oven models are equal – some will have three shelves and some will have four, or even five. To make things simple in this book, we like to describe them as "top", "middle" or "bottom" shelf. (You can see these racks on page 15, loaded with chicken drumsticks.)

can you cook directly on the racks?

Yes, you can. Think of the racks like an air fryer basket: ingredients to be air fried are often prepared in a bowl, then transferred to the basket. Instead, transfer the food to a rack, spreading it out so that it cooks evenly, and placing it at the top of the air fryer oven. Then, if an air fryer recipe asks you to "shake the basket", you would turn the food on the rack over with tongs instead.

If an air fryer basket recipe calls for using a silicone container, paper liner, foil or casserole dish, for example, because of the mess it makes, you can simply use a similar accessory and place the food on the rack in its container. As air fryer ovens are bigger, the advantage is that you can easily fit a 23cm/9 inch square container on a shelf in the oven, while in the air fryer basket the maximum you'll be able to fit is 18cm/7 inches.

air fryer oven accessories

Anything that you would use in the oven can be used in an air fryer oven, it will sometimes just need to be a bit smaller. Everything we have featured in this book for the basket or drawer can be used in the oven, but our favourite accessory for the oven is the mini oven tray. The ones we have measure 24cm x 18cm/9½ x 7 inches and we have used them in both the pork tenderloin traybake (see page 64) and the shrimp boil tray-bake (see page 66).

Not only are they great fun when used for one-person traybakes, but mini trays are also more convenient than many other accessories. Because the gap between the shelves isn't very high, if cooking on two shelves you sometimes won't be able to fit two foil trays in at once. The same issue would apply to casserole dishes, and deeper silicone pans, but the trays have low sides so prevent this being a problem.

the 20 per cent rule

After experimenting with the recipes from this book, we have found that air fryer ovens, on average, cook 20 per cent slower than basket or dual models. We cooked the same recipes in the basket or drawer air fryers at the same time as the oven and found that the food in the oven was not quite there – it wasn't generally as cooked or crispy and would need a little longer.

While the recipes in this chapter have been written for the oven and so no adjustments are necessary, if you would like to cook any of the other recipes in this book in an oven model, you will need to add about 20 per cent more cooking time. For example, if a basket recipe states 20 minutes, you will need to preheat the air fryer oven for 2 minutes, then cook the food on the rack for 25 minutes. Similarly, 8 minutes becomes 10 minutes, or 12 minutes becomes 15 minutes, and so on.

for even cooking

If you are only cooking enough food to fill one shelf, it doesn't matter where in the oven that shelf is situated. This is because the air fryer oven is small and the heat circulates very well.

But if you have a full layer of food on the top shelf (especially if it's on a tray or in a container), and wish to cook more on the middle or bottom shelf, any food below the top shelf will cook more slowly. The solution is to switch the shelves around during cooking, so that the food on both shelves is exposed to the heat at the top – see our pork tenderloin and shrimp boil recipes, where each tray gets time on the top shelf and you don't have a problem with uneven cooking. If you want foods to crisp up more, make sure they are at the top.

let's convert a recipe for the air fryer oven

If you are cooking a basket or dual recipe in the air fryer oven, follow the tips below for the best results:

- If you can cook food directly on the rack rather than using a container, do this, as the air will circulate more freely and not slow the cooking time of the food below as much (and may even add tasty cooking juices to the food below!).
- If everything will fit on one shelf, just use one shelf so that nothing is placed below.
- Preheat the air fryer oven for a couple of minutes before you add your food.
- If you are cooking one shelf of food, add 20 per cent of the cook time.
- If you are cooking two shelves of food, remember to switch them around during cooking so that the food on both the trays can crisp up, and add a little more cooking time on top of the 20 per cent.

Next, we are going to share with you how to cook a traybake in the air fryer oven, then introduce you to our favourite air fryer oven feature – the rotisserie.

pork tenderloin traybake

This is one of the first recipes we made using the air fryer oven. We loaded one mini oven tray with pork tenderloin and skin-on apples and pears, then the other with cubed root vegetables. Because the vegetables are cubed, it speeds up the cooking time.

....

SERVES **2**
HERO **OVEN**
PREP **10 MINUTES**
COOK TIME **55 MINUTES**
CALORIES **892**

....

1 × 450g/1lb pork tenderloin
1 red apple
1 pear
2 tbsp clear honey
1 tbsp wholegrain mustard
1 tsp garlic purée
2 tsp balsamic vinegar

FOR THE VEGETABLES
2 medium white potatoes
2 medium carrots
1 medium parsnip
140g/5oz Brussels sprouts
1 tbsp extra virgin olive oil
2 tsp dried thyme
Salt and black pepper

01 Scrub and peel the potatoes, carrots and parsnip, then dice them into 2cm/¾ inch cubes. Halve the spouts if large, or leave them whole if smaller. Put the vegetables in a bowl and add the olive oil and thyme. Add a generous seasoning of salt and pepper, and mix well with your hands.

02 Spread the root vegetables across one of the mini baking trays – leaving the sprouts in the bowl – and place on the top shelf of the air fryer oven. Set the temperature to 180ºC/360ºF and cook for 15 minutes. Add your sprouts and mix into the other vegetables, then cook for a further 10 minutes.

03 While the veg are cooking, place the pork tenderloin on the other baking tray, laying it diagonally so that it fits, and season generously with salt and pepper. Slice the apple and pear into wedges, discarding the cores. Spread the fruit out around the pork.

04 Put the honey, mustard, garlic purée and vinegar in a small bowl and mix with a tablespoon. Pour half the mixture over the pork and fruit, creating a glaze over the tops.

05 When the air fryer beeps, move the vegetable tray to a lower shelf and add the tray with the pork and fruit to the top shelf. Set the temperature to 180ºC/360ºF and cook for 30 minutes, or until the pork reaches an internal temperature of 70ºC/160ºF or above. Brush the pork with the remaining marinade, then serve the pork with the fruity wedges and the vegetables.

Dual or basket tenderloin If you are using the basket, you can add the pork tenderloin to the centre, then spread the fruit and veggies around the meat. Or if using a dual, you can place the pork tenderloin and fruit in one drawer and the vegetables in the other. Cook at 180ºC/360ºF for 28 minutes (matching the drawers if using a dual), adding the sprouts after the first 8 minutes.

Which trays? We use mini oven trays – you can see these on page 66, but you can use any tray that fits your air fryer oven.

shrimp boil traybake

A shrimp boil is a great simple traybake for your air fryer oven. If it's new to you, shrimp boil comes from the Deep South of the USA. It varies, but usually includes king prawns/ jumbo shrimp, smoked sausage, baby potatoes and mini corn on the cob. The Cajun seasoning and Cajun butter give it its wow factor.

SERVES **2**
HERO **OVEN**
PREP **15 MINUTES**
COOK TIME **39 MINUTES**
CALORIES **673**

....

4 frozen mini corn on the cob
1 large red onion
2 frankfurters/smoked
　sausages
4 baby potatoes
5 tsp Cajun seasoning
2 tsp garlic purée
Juice of ½ lemon
1 tbsp extra virgin olive oil
175g/6oz frozen raw peeled
　king prawns/shrimp
Salt and black pepper
　Fresh thyme leaves, for
　sprinkling
Lemon wedges, to serve

FOR THE CAJUN BUTTER SAUCE
55g/2oz/¼ cup salted butter
1 tsp Cajun seasoning
2 tsp garlic purée
1 tsp dried thyme
Juice of 1 lemon

01 Find yourself two air fryer oven trays (see page 63) and place two frozen corn on the cobs on each tray. Slice the red onion into slim wedges and divide them between the trays.

02 Slice the sausages and potatoes into quarters and put them in a mixing bowl. Add 3 teaspoons of the Cajun seasoning, the garlic purée, lemon juice and olive oil. Mix well, then arrange on the trays, drizzling any seasoned oil left in the bowl over the trays, too.

03 Put the trays in the air fryer oven, placing them on the top and bottom shelves, set the temperature to 180ºC/360ºF and cook for 10 minutes. Swap the trays around, and cook for another 10 minutes so that everything is evenly browned.

04 Remove the trays from the oven and scatter on the frozen prawns, spreading them evenly between the two trays. Sprinkle a teaspoon of the remaining Cajun seasoning over each tray, along with a generous seasoning of salt and pepper. Place the two trays back into the air fryer oven and cook at the same temperature for 16 minutes, swapping the trays around halfway through cooking, then remove the trays from the air fryer and set aside.

05 Add all the Cajun butter sauce ingredients to a ramekin. Place it in the oven and cook at the same temperature for 3 minutes, or until the butter has melted. Stir the sauce ingredients together, then pour it into two little sauce dishes and place a dish on each tray.

06 To serve, pour half the sauce over the ingredients on each tray, creating a delicious garlic sauce. Roll your corn on the cob in some of the butter and reserve the remaining sauce for dunking. Finish by sprinkling with fresh thyme and slicing two lemons into quarters creating lemon wedges and adding to the trays.

Basket or dual shrimp boil If using a basket or dual air fryer, the process is much quicker. First, cook the sausages and potatoes at 180ºC/360ºF for 10 minutes, then add the corn and the red onion and cook for another 10 minutes. Add the frozen prawns, stir, and cook for a final 10 minutes. If using the dual, split the ingredients between the two drawers for an even cook. We recommend cooking in a foil tray/pan so that it's easy to mix in the garlic butter and easier to serve.

let's learn all about the rotisserie

For many, the attraction of an air fryer oven is the rotisserie – and the ability to recreate your favourite rotisserie meat at home. A rod goes through the meat and clamps secure it in place so that the meat can constantly rotate. This means it's very juicy and never gets dry. You can use your imagination and do many combinations of meat, plus kebabs are also perfect this way.

honey mustard gammon

Whether you call it gammon or ham, it's our all-time favourite meat to cook using the rotisserie, and is a great rotisserie starting point.

1.2kg/2lb 10oz boneless gammon/ham joint
½ tsp black pepper
2 tsp dried parsley
2 tsp wholegrain mustard
2 tsp clear honey

SERVES **6**
HERO **OVEN**
PREP **5 MINUTES**
COOK TIME **65 MINUTES**
CALORIES **288**

01 Score both the fat side and lean side of the gammon with a knife going in by about 1cm/½in. This creates pockets to hold the seasonings to make your gammon more flavoursome.

02 Add the pepper, parsley, mustard and honey to a small bowl and mix with a fork. Using a pastry brush, brush the marinade all over the gammon, making sure it goes into the cuts you have made.

03 Push the rod all the way through the gammon joint until it comes out the other side.

04 Feed a clamp onto the rod, as far as it will go until the spikes of the clamp are firmly skewering the gammon. Repeat for the opposite end so that the gammon is clamped in place.

05 Position the gammon so that it is in the middle of the rod, then tighten the screws to finger tight.

06 Carefully place the gammon in the air fryer oven, positioning the rod in the rotisserie socket. Make sure that it is hooked in properly on both sides and that it won't fall off.

07 Set the temperature to 180ºC/360ºF and air fry the gammon for 65 minutes, or until the gammon reaches an internal temperature of 70ºC/160ºF or above.

Top tips

I'm watching you As you start the rotisserie, we recommend that you turn the light on and watch it for the first 2 minutes. This is to make sure that the rod is rotating properly in the socket.

Weight matters Because you're securing the meat on a rod that is rotating, it can't be too heavy or the meat will fall off. Aim for a joint that's between 800g/1¾lb and 1.3kg/3lb.

Attach to the meat When using the rotisserie, it's important that the spikes on the clamp are inserted firmly into the meat. This stops the meat from moving about and keeps it in position as it rotates.

Seasoning variety You can use any dried seasonings on your rotisserie meats; we recommend 1 tablespoon per whole chicken, or per roasting joint. Instead of 1 tablespoon of mixed herbs, you could add the same amount of Cajun seasoning, Chinese 5-spice, or why not make a piri piri chicken?

Mix a marinade If you would like to marinade your rotisserie meat, why not try one of the 7 marinades from page 37. You can prepare them ahead of time too, then cook when you are ready.

Rest, then remove We recommend removing the meat from the air fryer oven with oven gloves, then allow it to rest before removing the clamps and rod.

Love leftovers These rotisserie recipes will feed 4–6 people. Keep any leftovers in an airtight container in your fridge, then use the air fryer shelves to warm them up the next day. Or why not try the gammon in sandwiches, like we do in our afternoon tea on page 218?

brazilian picanha barbecue

If I could just eat one type of meat for the rest of my life, it would be the Brazilian picanha. Famous at Brazilian barbecue buffet restaurants, it is carved at your table and you just know you're going to ask the waiter for another slice. Back at home, the picanha can be recreated using the rotisserie.

....

SERVES **6**
HERO **OVEN**
PREP **5 MINUTES**
COOK TIME **35 MINUTES, PLUS RESTING**
CALORIES **388**

....

1.3kg/3lb rump beef (with fat cap attached)
Extra virgin olive oil spray
2 tsp garlic purée
2 tsp smoked paprika
1 tsp dried parsley
¼ tsp light brown sugar
¼ tsp onion powder
A pinch of cayenne pepper
1 tsp sea salt
1 tsp black pepper

01 Slice the rump in half, creating two separate pieces both with a piece of the rump cap attached. Thread the rod through the top of a rump piece, then bend the piece round and thread the rod back through the bottom of the piece too, to create a 'C' shape with the meat with the fat on the outside. Repeat for the second piece of rump, pushing them close together so that the two fit on the rod.

02 Lay the rod flat on a clean chopping board and spray the top half of the rump with olive oil, then smother with half the garlic purée, rubbing it into the olive oil with your fingertips.

03 Combine the paprika, parsley, sugar, onion powder, cayenne pepper, salt and black pepper in a small bowl, then sprinkle half over the top of the rump and rub it in with your hands. Turn the rump over and do the same again, spraying with the olive oil, smothering with the remaining garlic purée, then coating with the remaining rub and seasoning.

04 Feed a clamp through the end of the rod, as far as it will go until the spikes of the clamp are firmly skewering the beef. Repeat to add a clamp on the opposite side, so that the rump is secured in place.

05 Position the rump steaks so that they are in the middle of the rod. Once in the middle, tighten the screws to finger tight.

06 Carefully place the rump in the air fryer oven, positioning the rod in the rotisserie socket. Make sure that it is hooked in properly on both sides and that it won't fall off.

07 Set the temperature to 180°C/360°F and air fry the rump beef for 35 minutes for medium-rare. Remove from the air fryer oven with oven gloves, then allow it to rest for 5 minutes before serving.

Dual or basket Brazilian beef Half this rump will fit in an air fryer basket – just halve the seaosning mix – or you can fit one half in each drawer of a dual. Place each half on a metal kebab skewer and spread half the seasoning across each piece of rump. Cook at 180°C/360°F for 30 minutes.

Brazilian barbecue cook times
Cook at 180°C/360°F for:
25 minutes – rare
35 minutes – medium-rare
40 minutes – medium
50 minutes – medium-well done
60 minutes – well done

apple cider pork shoulder

We always associate pork shoulder with the slow cooker and pulled pork. But a delicious plan B is to use the rotisserie to air fry pork shoulder. When carved, it's a delicious pork roast that is perfect for your next roast dinner.

SERVES **6**
HERO **OVEN**
PREP **5 MINUTES**
COOK TIME **60 MINUTES**
CALORIES **490**

1.2kg/2lb 10oz boneless pork shoulder
440ml/15½fl oz/1¾ cups sweet (hard) apple cider
1 tbsp extra virgin olive oil
1 tbsp sweet paprika
Salt and black pepper

01 Place the pork shoulder in a large mixing bowl and pour over the apple cider. Cover with cling film/plastic wrap and place in the fridge to marinate for at least 2 hours, although you can leave it overnight if you prefer.

02 After marinating, remove the pork shoulder from the cider, then use kitchen paper/paper towel to pat it dry. Drizzle the olive oil over the shoulder, sprinkle with sweet paprika and season with salt and pepper. Use your hands to rub the olive oil and seasonings into the pork.

03 Push the rod all the way through the pork shoulder until it comes out the other side.

04 Feed a clamp onto the rod, as far as it will go until the spikes of the clamp are firmly skewering the pork. Then repeat for the opposite end so that the pork is clamped in place.

05 Position the pork so that it is in the middle of the rod. Once in the middle, tighten the screws to finger tight.

06 Carefully place the pork in the air fryer oven, positioning the rod in the rotisserie socket. Make sure that it is hooked in properly on both sides and that it won't fall off.

07 Set the temperature to 180ºC/360ºF and air fry the pork for 60 minutes, or until the pork reaches an internal temperature of 70ºC/160ºF or above.

Basket or dual pork If you don't have an air fryer with a rotisserie function, you can follow the recipe above for pork (or the gammon recipe on page 68) and convert it for cooking in an air fryer basket or in a dual air fryer. Prepare the pork as above, but instead of a rod and clamps, place the joint into the air fryer basket (or drawer). Set the temperature to 180ºC/360ºF and air fry for 25 minutes. Turn the pork over and air fry at the same temperature for another 25 minutes, or until cooked through.

rotisserie chicken

I have lost count of the amount of times I have queued in the supermarket for a rotisserie chicken. The excitement when they pass you the bag with the warm chicken inside! But I have not bought a single one since I got an air fryer XL. I buy a chicken from my local butcher and can cook the whole chicken in the basket or watch it rotate on the rotisserie

....

SERVES **4**
HERO **OVEN**
PREP **5 MINUTES**
COOK TIME **50 MINUTES**
CALORIES **470**

....

1.3kg/3lb medium whole chicken
1 tbsp extra virgin olive oil
1 tbsp mixed herbs/Italian seasoning
Salt and black pepper

01 Place the whole chicken on a clean chopping board. Drizzle with olive oil and sprinkle over the mixed herbs and a generous seasoning of salt and pepper. Use your hands to rub the olive oil and seasonings all over the chicken.

02 Tie the chicken legs with string, then push the rod all the way through the chicken until it comes out the other side.

03 Feed a clamp onto the rod, as far as it will go until the spikes of the clamp are firmly skewering the chicken. Repeat for the opposite end so that the bird is clamped in place. Make sure the clamp is attached to chicken meat, not the bone.

04 Position the chicken so that it is in the middle of the rod. Once in the middle, tighten the screws to finger tight.

05 Carefully place the chicken in the air fryer oven, positioning the rod in the rotisserie socket. Make sure that it is hooked in properly on both sides and that it won't fall off.

06 Set the temperature to 180°C/360°F and air fry the chicken for 50 minutes, or until the chicken reaches an internal temperature of 70°C/160°F or above.

Basket or dual chicken Prepare the chicken as above. But instead of a rod and clamps, place the chicken directly into the air fryer basket/drawer, breast side down. Set the temperature to 180°C/360°F and air fry for 25 minutes. Turn the chicken over and air fry at the same temperature for another 25 minutes, or until the chicken reaches an internal temperature of 70°C/160°F or above. You can also do the same with the roast duck and other similar-sized birds, although if you like your duck a little pink, reduce the cook time by 10 minutes.

Pair of poussins Another favourite trick of ours is air frying two poussins together using the rotisserie. Known in the USA as a Cornish hen, they are small spring chickens and they air fry so well. You can do just one, or two like we do. Simply follow the rotisserie chicken recipe above, but divide the oil and seasonings between two 450g/1lb poussins, then feed them both onto the rod. Use the same temperature, but because they are much smaller air fry for 25 minutes, or until the chicken reaches an internal temperature of 70°C/160°F or above.

crispy duck & pancakes

The first food I ever tried at a Chinese restaurant was crispy duck and pancakes. It's now my go-to when I order a Chinese takeaway, but you can do it at home – much cheaper – in the air fryer.

....

SERVES **4**
HERO **OVEN**
PREP **5 MINUTES**
COOK TIME **45 MINUTES**
CALORIES **302**

....

1 tsp garlic purée
½ tsp ginger purée
2 tbsp clear honey
½ tbsp soy sauce
3 tbsp oyster sauce
1.2kg/2lb 10oz whole duck
1 tbsp extra virgin olive oil
1 tbsp Chinese 5-spice powder
12 Chinese pancakes
½ cucumber
a few spring onions/scallions
Salt and black pepper

01 In a small bowl, combine the garlic and ginger purées, honey, soy sauce and oyster sauce. Set half aside in another bowl for serving.

02 Use a knife to create score slashes across the skin of the duck breast, cutting through the fat but making sure you don't pierce the flesh so it stays juicy. Drizzle the duck with olive oil, sprinkle with the Chinese 5-spice and season with salt and pepper. Rub the seasonings into the duck with your hands until it's evenly coated.

03 Next, coat the duck with the sauce using a pastry brush, making sure you cover it completely.

04 Tie up the duck legs with string, then push the rod all the way through the duck until it comes out the other side. Feed a clamp onto the rod until the spikes of the clamp are firmly skewering the duck. Repeat for the opposite end so that the bird is clamped in place. Make sure the clamp is attached to duck meat, not the bone.

05 Position the duck so that it is in the middle of the rod. Once in the middle, tighten the screws. Carefully place the duck in the air fryer oven, positioning the rod in the rotisserie socket. Make sure that it is hooked in properly on both sides and that it won't fall off.

06 Set the temperature to 180°C/360°F and air fry the duck for 45 minutes, or until the duck reaches an internal temperature of 60°C/140°F or above, depending how you like your duck. Remove the duck from the rod and allow it to cool before carving.

07 While the duck is resting, make your crispy duck platter. Add the reserved sauce to a bowl, get out your pancakes and slice your cucumber and spring onion into thin matchsticks.

08 Once the duck is cool enough to handle, shred the duck. Pile it onto a serving platter with the pancakes, cucumber and spring onion and serve with the sauce on the side. Everyone can help themselves, filling the pancakes with a layer of the sauce, shredded duck, cucumber and spring onion, then an extra drizzle of the sauce.

Crispy duck After cooking the duck, you're likely to be shredding the duck for pancakes. The skin will be nice and crispy, but if you want the meat crispy too, this can be done quickly in the air fryer. After shredding, spray the meat with olive oil and add it to the top shelf of the air fryer oven, or put it in the air fryer basket, and air fry at 200°C/400°F for 8 minutes. You can also do the same with your duck leftovers.

Save the duck fat As the duck rotates, the lovely fat will drip down into the drip tray at the bottom of the air fryer oven. When the air fryer is cool enough to handle, carefully remove the drip tray and tip the duck fat into a mesh strainer set over an airtight container (with a lid). Strain the fat into the container, then pop on the lid and keep in the fridge, ready for your next batch of air fried potatoes.

greek gyros

One of the rotisserie's magic tricks is kebabs. Because it is rotating, you never have to worry about the meat getting dry. Let's start with these yummy gyros, served in flatbreads with French fries and plenty of Greek sauce.

....

SERVES **6**
HERO **OVEN**
PREP **15 MINUTES, PLUS MARINATING**
COOK TIME **60 MINUTES**
CALORIES **642**

....

900g/2lb boneless skinless chicken thighs

FOR THE GYRO MARINADE
2 tsp garlic purée
1 tbsp balsamic vinegar
1 tbsp lemon juice
1 tbsp extra virgin olive oil
2 tbsp thick Greek yoghurt
2 tsp dried oregano
Salt and black pepper

FOR THE GREEK SAUCE
Juice of 1 small lemon
½ tsp garlic purée
5 tbsp thick Greek yoghurt
A pinch of dried parsley

TO SERVE
6 Saskia's Flatbreads (see page 196), warmed
1 recipe quantity French Fries (see page 154)
Shredded lettuce
1 medium cucumber, diced
1 large tomato, chopped

01 Put the marinade ingredients in a bowl and mix well. Add the chicken thighs and mix well with your hands. Cover the bowl with cling film/plastic wrap and place in the fridge to marinate for at least 2 hours, but overnight is best.

02 After marinating, remove the cling film and feed all the chicken thighs onto the rod. You will have to push them down close to each other for them all to fit.

03 Feed a clamp onto the rod, as far as it will go until the spikes of the clamp are firmly skewering the chicken meat. Then repeat for the opposite end so that all the chicken is clamped in place.

04 Position the chicken so that it is centred in the middle of the rod and not too close to the edges. Once in the middle, tighten the screws to finger tight.

05 Carefully place the marinated chicken in the air fryer oven, positioning the rod in the rotisserie socket. Make sure that it is hooked in properly on both sides and that it won't fall off.

06 Set the temperature to 180°C/360°F and air fry the chicken for 30 minutes. Reduce the temperature to 160°C/320°F and air fry for another 30 minutes or until the chicken reaches an internal temperature of 70°C/160°F or above. Use oven gloves to remove the chicken rod from the air fryer oven.

07 Whilst the gyro meat is air frying, put the Greek sauce ingredients in a bowl, mix to combine and set aside.

08 Once the gyro meat has rested, you can slice it directly from the rod and it will slice like a kebab from the takeaway. Pile the gyro meat into warm flatbreads along with fries and salad, and finish with a drizzle of the Greek sauce.

Basket or dual gyros Using a metal kebab holder that fits the size of your air fryer, place half the gyro meat on the rod and place in the air fryer basket. Set the temperature to 180°C/360°F and air fry for 20 minutes. Turn the kebab over and cook at the lower temperature of 160°C/320°F for another 20 minutes. Repeat for the remaining gyro meat, or if you have a dual fryer you can do one in each drawer.

rotisserie kebabs (three ways)

Beyond using the rod and clamps you also have a kebab holder. We recommend cooking five kebabs at once. They rotate like a rotisserie, and we love to mix and match between the kebabs below. If cooking in batches, start tucking into one while the next is cooking.

tofu kebabs

Tofu cubes, courgette and cherry tomatoes with a delicious dried Greek rub make an easy vegan alternative to our gyros from page 77.

....

MAKES **5**
HERO **OVEN**
PREP **5 MINUTES**
COOK TIME **15 MINUTES**
CALORIES **113**

....

¾ medium courgette/zucchini
225g/8oz block of tofu, pressed (see page 145)
170g/6oz cherry tomatoes
1 tbsp extra virgin olive oil
1 tbsp balsamic vinegar
1 tsp lemon juice
2 tsp dried oregano
½ tsp dried rosemary
1 tsp mixed herbs/Italian seasoning
½ tsp garlic powder
Salt and black pepper

01 Slice the courgette into 2cm/¾ inch thick slices, then cut the slices in half. Cut the tofu into 2cm/¾ inch cubes and put them in a bowl with the cherry tomatoes and courgette. Add the olive oil, balsamic vinegar, lemon juice, dried herbs and garlic powder. Season generously with salt and pepper, then mix well with your hands.

02 Very gently thread the cubed tofu, sliced courgette and whole cherry tomatoes onto the kebab skewers, dividing the different elements equally between the five skewers. Attach the kebab holder to the rotisserie rod and hook the skewers onto the kebab holder. Position the

rod in the rotisserie socket, making sure that it is hooked in properly on both sides and that it won't fall off.

03 Set the temperature to 180°C/360°F and cook for 15 minutes, or until crispy to your liking. Or if you prefer crispier tofu, add an extra 5 minutes of cooking time at the same temperature.

Pork and halloumi souvlaki Pork steak with halloumi and Greek seasoning also makes a delicious summery air fryer kebab. Put **340g/12oz pork steak** and **175g/6oz halloumi cheese** (both diced into 2.5cm/1 inch cubes) into a bowl. Add **1 tbsp white wine vinegar, 2 tbsp extra virgin olive oil, 2 tsp lemon juice, 2 tsp garlic purée, 2 tsp wholegrain mustard, 2 tsp dried rosemary, 2 tsp dried oregano and 2 tsp sweet paprika**, season with **salt and black pepper** and mix well. Gently thread the halloumi and pork onto the kebab skewers. Cook at 180°C/360°F for 18 minutes, or until the pork is cooked through and the halloumi is turning light golden.

Surf and turf This is my all-time favourite kebab, combining steak with prawns/shrimp. Make as the kebabs above, but instead of tofu, slice **310g/11oz steak** into chunks, then thaw **225g/8oz raw king prawns/shrimp**. Add both to a bowl with **1 teaspoon steak seasoning** and **1 tablespoon extra virgin olive oil** and season well with **salt and pepper**. Mix well with your hands and feed onto the kebab skewers. Air fry at 180°C/360°F for 8 minutes.

Basket or dual kebabs Thread the tofu, pork, halloumi or prawns/shrimp onto smaller metal skewers, which will fit in the air fryer basket or into the drawers. Set the temperature to 180°C/360°F and air fry for 12 minutes, turning halfway through, until cooked through.

POULTRY

Let's air fry a poussin

One of the biggest mistakes people make when buying an air fryer is getting one that is too small. The assumption is that if you are feeding one to two people, you just need a small one. Then you realise how amazing it would be to cook a whole chicken in it and realise you went too small.

That is when a poussin (known in the USA as a Cornish hen) becomes a wonderful plan B.

They weigh on average between 450g/1lb and 650g/1lb 7oz, making them a third of the weight – and a much smaller size – than a standard chicken. This means that they cook much faster in the air fryer, as well as being a perfect fit for the tiny air fryer, or for those with a smaller appetite.

piri piri poussin with fries

In Portugal, the famous piri piri chicken is always made with small chickens, served with French fries and a side salad or rice. We're going to show you how to do this with a poussin and how you can combine the poussin with the fries in a small air fryer basket.

1 tbsp dried piri piri seasoning
½ tbsp lemon juice
½ tbsp garlic purée
2 tbsp extra virgin olive oil
1 × 450/1lb poussin/Cornish hen

FOR THE FRENCH FRIES
2 medium white potatoes
2 tsp extra virgin olive oil
1 tsp dried coriander/cilantro leaf
Salt and black pepper

SERVES **1**
HERO **SMALL BASKET**
PREP **10 MINUTES**
COOK TIME **40 MINUTES**
CALORIES **1253**

01 Put the piri piri seasoning, lemon juice, garlic purée and olive oil in a small bowl and mix with a spoon. Place the poussin, breast side down, on a chopping board, then smoother half the marinade mixture over any visible skin.

02 Next, slice the potatoes into French fries, leaving the skins on. Put them in a bowl and add the olive oil, coriander and a generous seasoning of salt and pepper. Mix with your hands until the fries are well coated, then scatter the fries into the air fryer basket, adding them to the gaps around the outside of the poussin. Set the temperature to 180°C/360°F and air fry for 20 minutes.

03 When the air fryer beeps, turn the poussin over by positioning a fork inside its cavity and flipping it. Use a pastry brush to brush the remaining marinade over the other half of the poussin, again covering all visible skin.

04 Continue air frying at the same temperature for a further 15 minutes, or until the poussin reaches an internal temperature of 70°C/160°F or above. Remove the poussin from the basket and put it to one side to rest.

05 Shake the air fryer basket and the juices from the poussin will mix with the French fries for a lovely flavour. Air fry at the same temperature for an extra 5 minutes to make the fries crispier.

06 When the air fryer beeps, quarter the poussin, creating four pieces of poultry, and serve with the fries.

Top tips

Have a bigger air fryer? The beauty of the poussin is that you can fit one in a small air fryer and two in a bigger air fryer, whilst keeping the same time and temperature. If you have a dual, you can cook a poussin in one drawer, then fries in the other, or why not try two poussins on the rotisserie? (See page 73.)

Don't like piri piri? Swap the piri piri for 1 tablespoon of another favourite dried seasoning.

Add a salad The Portuguese make a delicious salad to go with their piri piri baby chickens, with little gem lettuce and sliced cucumber, onion and tomato. They toss it in a dressing of 2 teaspoons each of honey, olive oil, balsamic vinegar and white wine vinegar.

hunter's chicken

What is not to love about hunter's chicken? This classic dish of chicken breast, wrapped in bacon, smothered in barbecue sauce, and topped with melted cheese is made so easy with the air fryer. We use a silicone container to avoid a big clean up, or you can use paper liners.

SERVES **4**
HERO **BASKET/DUAL**
PREP **5 MINUTES**
COOK TIME **33 MINUTES**
CALORIES **539**

4 medium chicken breasts
8 rashers smoked back bacon
55g/2oz/heaped ½ cup grated mature/sharp Cheddar cheese
55g/2oz/½ cup grated mozzarella cheese
Salt and black pepper

FOR THE BARBECUE SAUCE
240ml/8fl oz/1 cup barbecue sauce
4 tbsp clear honey
1 tsp garlic purée
2 tsp sweet paprika

01 Put your chicken breasts onto a chopping board and season generously with salt and pepper. Tightly wrap two slices of bacon around each chicken breast, covering it well. Secure the bacon with cocktail sticks/toothpicks to stop it flying off during air frying.

02 Gently place the bacon-wrapped chicken breasts in the air fryer basket/drawer. Set the temperature to 180ºC/360ºF and air fry for 28 minutes, or until the chicken reads an internal temperature of 70ºC/160ºF or above.

03 While the chicken is air frying, add all the barbecue sauce ingredients to an air fryer-safe dish or silicone pan, and mix with a fork.

04 When the air fryer beeps, remove the chicken from the air fryer and remove the cocktail sticks that have held the bacon in place.

05 Place the chicken in the dish so that it's sitting in the barbecue sauce, then sprinkle both the grated cheeses over the chicken.

06 Air fry the hunter's chicken at 180ºC/360ºF for a final 5 minutes to melt the cheese and warm up the barbecue sauce before serving.

sweet chilli chicken breasts with cucumber noodles

We love sweet chilli chicken. Because of the sweet chilli marinade the chicken gets a slightly chargrilled look and tastes so flavoursome. Serve with cucumber noodles and it's a delicious light summer meal.

SERVES **2**
HERO **BASKET/DUAL**
PREP **8 MINUTES**
COOK TIME **20 MINUTES**
CALORIES **404**

2 Sweet Chilli marinated
  medium chicken breasts
  (see page 37)
1 cucumber
¼ tsp Chinese 5-spice powder
1 tbsp extra virgin olive oil
1 tsp garlic purée
½ tsp ginger purée
½ tsp lemongrass purée
Salt and black pepper
Sliced red chilli, to serve
  (optional)

01 Line the air fryer basket/drawer with a paper liner or a foil tray, then add the marinated sweet chilli chicken breasts. Pour any extra marinade from the bag over the chicken, too. Set the temperature to 180°C/360°F and cook for 20 minutes.

02 Whilst the chicken is cooking, make your cucumber noodles. Peel the cucumber with a potato peeler or julienne peeler to make thin ribbons or noodles. Squeeze the cucumber between your hands to release excess moisture, then place in a bowl and add all the remaining ingredients. Mix well to coat the cucumber noodles in the dressing, then split the noodles between two dinner plates.

03 When the air fryer beeps, use a thermometer to check if the chicken is 70°C/160°F or above. If not, cook for an extra 4 minutes and check again. Allow it to rest for a few minutes, then slice it and serve with the cucumber noodles, scattered with red chilli if you like some extra heat.

sofia's dorito wings

MAKES **8**
HERO **BASKET/DUAL**
PREP **8 MINUTES**
COOK TIME **20 MINUTES**
CALORIES **340**

1 × 180g/6¼oz Doritos, or other
  tortilla chips
2 large eggs
35g/1¼oz/¼ cup plain/all-
  purpose flour
8 large chicken wings
1 tbsp sweet paprika
1 tsp garlic powder
Extra virgin olive oil spray
Salt and black pepper
Sour cream and chive dip, to
  serve (optional)

Crispy air-fried chicken wings are delicious and there are so many different ways to coat them. This wings recipe was made by Sofia, who loved bashing the bag of Doritos into the perfect crumb.

01 Thoroughly bash the bag of Doritos with a rolling pin until they are in fine crumbs, then transfer them to a bowl.

02 Crack the eggs into another bowl and season with salt and pepper, then beat the eggs with a fork. Put the flour in a third bowl. Arrange the bowls in a production line, starting with the flour, then the egg, then the Dorito crumbs.

03 Place the chicken wings on a chopping board and season generously with salt and pepper. Sprinkle the paprika and garlic powder evenly onto the wings and use your hands to rub the seasonings all over them.

04 One at a time, dunk the wings first into the flour, then drench in the egg, then roll them in the Dorito crumbs, making sure the wings get a good coating from each.

05 Place the wings in the air fryer basket/drawer and spread out. If using a dual fryer, you can spread them out over two drawers. You may need to cook them in two batches. Set the temperature to 180ºC/360ºF and cook for 20 minutes until golden and crispy, spraying with olive oil halfway through for a better crisp, then serve – with sour cream and chive dip, if you like.

apricot chicken dinner for two

The clever "sync" feature on the dual means that different foods will be ready at the same time, even if they have different cooking times. We will be cooking the marinated vegetables in one drawer and the chicken legs in the other for a lovely dinner in for two.

SERVES **2**
HERO **DUAL**
PREP **8 MINUTES**
COOK TIME **25 MINUTES**
CALORIES **726**

½ yellow (bell) pepper/capsicum
½ orange (bell) pepper/ capsicum
1 medium courgette/zucchini
6 dried apricots
175g/6oz cherry tomatoes
½ x 400g/14oz can chickpeas, drained
2 heaped tsp ground cumin
2 tsp smoked paprika
2 medium chicken legs
Salt and black pepper
fresh coriander/cilantro leaves, to serve

FOR THE APRICOT MARINADE
145g/5oz/½ cup apricot jam
1 tbsp white wine vinegar
1 tbsp extra virgin olive oil
2 tsp garlic purée
2 tsp ginger purée
2 tsp harissa paste
2 tsp ground cumin
1 tbsp dried coriander/cilantro leaf

01 Put all the apricot marinade ingredients in a bowl and mix well. If you have a really thick jam, use the back of the spoon to break it down. Set aside.

02 Dice the peppers into 2cm/¾ inch chunks. Slice the courgette into 2cm/¾ inch thick slices, then cut the slices into quarters. Slice the dried apricots into quarters. Put the pepper, courgette, apricots and cherry tomatoes into a bowl. Add the chickpeas, cumin and smoked paprika, along with three-quarters of the apricot marinade, and mix everything together well with your hands. Place the vegetables in one drawer of your dual without the crisper plate.

03 Season the chicken legs generously with salt and pepper, then coat them in the remaining marinade. Place the chicken legs in the second drawer, leaving the crisper plate in this time.

04 Once you have a drawer ready with the vegetables and a second drawer with the chicken, it's time to sync your air fryer drawers. Press "sync" then set the vegetable drawer to air fry at 180ºC/360ºF for 25 minutes, then set the chicken drawer to the same temperature for 20 minutes. The chicken will start cooking once 5 minutes has passed, so that they will both be ready at the same time. Though, for an even cook, we recommend for the last 5 minutes that you use tongs to turn the chicken over.

05 Transfer the vegetables to a serving platter and top with the chicken, then scatter with coriander leaves and serve.

Apricot chicken in a basket To cook in the basket simply use a container that will fit your air fryer and keep the same time and temperature. Then place the chicken over the vegetables and it can all cook together.

Plan ahead If you prefer to make ahead, you can place the chicken into the bowl over the vegetables, wrap in cling film/plastic wrap and leave to marinate in the fridge until you're ready to cook.

turkey dinner for one

At Christmas, Thanksgiving and Easter, everyone prepares massive meals, but what if you're just cooking for one? For this hearty turkey dinner, we use a single turkey steak, serving it with a stuffing ball, pigs in blankets, roast potatoes and veggie fries. Rather than buying large packs from the supermarket, we purchase meat from our local butchers and vegetables from the greengrocer, which means we can order smaller portions – perfect for feeding one.

....

SERVES **1**
HERO **BASKET/DUAL**
PREP **10 MINUTES**
COOK TIME **34 MINUTES**
CALORIES **984**

....

1 medium parsnip
1 medium turnip
1 medium carrot
1 medium white potato
1 tbsp extra virgin olive oil
1 heaped tsp dried parsley
225g/8oz turkey steak
1 tsp dried thyme
1 sage and onion stuffing ball
  (see tip opposite)
2 pigs in blankets (mini
  sausages wrapped in streaky
  bacon)
240ml (8fl oz/1 cup) turkey gravy
Salt and black pepper
Cranberry sauce, to serve
  (optional)

01 Peel the parsnip, turnip and carrots, then slice them into vegetable sticks. Peel the potato and cut it into quarters. Put all the veg in a mixing bowl and season generously with salt and pepper. Add the olive oil and parsley, and mix well with your hands so that they are well coated in the oil and seasonings.

02 Remove the potatoes from the bowl and put them into the air fryer basket/drawer. Set the temperature to 180ºC/360ºF and air fry for 5 minutes to give the potatoes a head-start. Once the 5 minutes is up, add the remaining vegetables and cook for a further 15 minutes.

03 When the air fryer beeps, shake, and do a fork test – skewer a carrot or two with a fork and if it feels like they are almost tender, it's time to add the meat. Move the potatoes and vegetables to one side of the basket to make room for the turkey. If you are using a dual fryer, use the second drawer for the meat.

04 Season the turkey steak with salt and pepper and sprinkle the thyme over it. Add it to the air fryer and find another gap for the stuffing ball and the pigs in blankets. Air fry at the same temperature for another 12 minutes, flipping the steak after 8 minutes.

05 Add the turkey steak, potatoes and vegetables to a dinner plate. Tip the gravy into a ramekin and place this into the gap you've just made in the air fryer. Air fry at 200ºC/400ºF for 2 minutes; this will crisp up the pigs in blankets and the stuffing ball, as well as heating the gravy through. Add the remaining items to your plate and serve. We love to add a generous spoonful of cranberry sauce to compliment the turkey.

Single stuffing balls Many butchers will sell you an individual stuffing ball, but if you can't get them, simply buy a pack, remove one and freeze the remainder. Then, when you are cooking a Sunday roast for one in the future, you can just remove another from the freezer as you need it.

teriyaki duck noodles

One of our go-to air fryer ingredients is egg noodles. Compared to pasta or rice, they are fast cooking in the air fryer. You can combine your favourite protein (in this recipe we are using duck breast) with a simple sticky Asian sauce and a stir fry vegetable mix. Super-simple and perfect for busy weeknights.

....

SERVES **2**
HERO **BASKET/DUAL**
PREP **8 MINUTES**
COOK TIME **25 MINUTES**
CALORIES **1450**

....

2 × 225g/8oz skin-on duck
   breasts
1 tbsp extra virgin olive oil
½ tsp Chinese 5-spice powder
Salt and black pepper

FOR THE TERIYAKI SAUCE
2 × 120g/4¼oz pouches thick
   teriyaki sauce
1 tsp ginger purée
2 tsp garlic purée
A splash of soy sauce

FOR THE STIR FRY
2 spring onions/scallions
300g/10½oz stir fry vegetable
   mix (we use a mix with carrot,
   green cabbage, bean sprouts,
   red (bell) pepper/capsicum
   and water chestnuts)
1 tsp Chinese 5-spice powder
1 tbsp extra virgin olive oil
½ x 275g/9¾oz pack of fresh
   egg noodles

01 Place the duck breasts, skin-side down, into the air fryer basket/drawer. Rub the tops of the duck with half the olive oil, sprinkle with the Chinese 5-spice powder, and season generously with salt and pepper. Set the temperature to 180ºC/360ºF and air fry for 5 minutes.

02 Mix all the teriyaki sauce ingredients together in a small bowl. When the air fryer beeps, flip the duck over with tongs and season the skin side with salt and pepper. Brush about ½ tablespoon of the teriyaki sauce over each duck breast using a pastry brush. Air fry the duck at the same temperature for a further 7 minutes, then remove it from the air fryer and allow it to rest.

03 For the stir fry, slice the spring onions and set the green parts aside. Put the spring onions whites and the stir fry vegetables in a mixing bowl and add the Chinese 5-spice powder and the olive oil. Season with salt and pepper and mix well with your hands. Tip the stir fry mix into the air fryer basket/drawer and spread it out. Air fry at 180ºC/360ºF for 8 minutes, or until the stir fry mix is starting to get crispy.

04 Put the remaining teriyaki sauce and the egg noodles into a silicone pan with handles. Once done, add the stir fry vegetables and use a fork to mix everything together so that the noodles and veggies are evenly coated in the sauce.

05 Place the silicone pan into the air fryer basket and air fry at 180ºC/360ºF for a final 5 minutes, or until the egg noodles are heated through.

06 Slice the duck breasts and serve them on top of the stir fried teriyaki noodles, sprinkled with the spring onion greens.

Dual noodles If you have the dual air fryer, speed up the cook time by cooking the stir fry mix in one drawer and the duck breasts in the other drawer.

MEAT

Let's air fry a beef wellington

Succulent fillet of beef surrounded by a flavoursome layer of prosciutto, pâté and garlic mushrooms, all covered with crisp, golden pastry is the ultimate dinner party favourite. It first became popular to cook beef Wellington's in the air fryer back in 2018, and it's easier than you think to prepare, but before you start, see our tips on page 100.

special occasion beef wellington

SERVES **6**
HERO **BASKET**
PREP **20 MINUTES**
COOK TIME **84 MINUTES**
CALORIES **523**

....

900g/2lb beef fillet
Extra virgin olive oil spray
2 tsp dried thyme
2 tsp dried parsley
250g/9oz chestnut (cremini) mushrooms
A pinch of garlic powder
Plain (all-purpose) flour, for dusting
1 × 500g/1lb 2oz pack of puff pastry
100g/3½oz prosciutto slices
180g/6¼oz Brussels pâté
1 egg, beaten
Salt and black pepper

01 Place your fillet on a chopping board, spray with olive oil, then rub the herbs and salt and pepper all over the fillet. Air fry at 180ºC/360ºF for 5 minutes, flip over and cook at the same temperature for another 5 minutes. Allow to rest and, once cool, wrap in foil and put in the fridge overnight. The next day, remove the fillet from the fridge, unwrap the foil and pat it dry with kitchen paper/paper towel.

02 Slice the mushrooms into 5mm/¼ inch slices and tip them into the air fryer basket. Spray with olive oil and season with salt, pepper and garlic powder. Set the temperature to 180ºC/360ºF and cook for 9 minutes. Tip the mushrooms onto a plate to cool.

03 Flour a clean worktop and your rolling pin, and roll out the puff pastry to a large rectangle measuring about 35 × 28cm/14 × 11 inches. Lay your prosciutto slices over the pastry, leaving a 1cm/½ inch border around the edge, then spread an even layer of pâté over the prosciutto. Add a layer of the cold sliced mushrooms over the pâté, overlapping them so that there are no gaps. Place the fillet of beef over the mushrooms in the centre of the pastry sheet. Using a pastry brush, brush a layer of egg wash over the border around the edge of the pastry. Carefully roll the pastry over to create a tight log, tucking in the pastry at the sides as you go.

04 Poke holes in a paper air fryer liner so that the air can circulate (this is important so that it doesn't slow down the cooking time) and place the liner in the air fryer basket. Carefully place the Wellington into the air fryer basket over the paper liner, with the seal side upwards (and best side down – you'll flip it later), and brush the top with egg wash. Cook at 180ºC/360ºF for 20 minutes.

05 Use the sides of the paper liner as handles to help you lift the Wellington out of the air fryer onto a worktop. Carefully roll it over, so that it's now the right way up and place back onto the paper liner. Cut small slits in the pastry along the top of the Wellington to let the steam escape so that the pastry won't go soggy. Use the liner again to carefully place the Wellington back into the air fryer basket and brush the top and sides with extra egg wash. Set the temperature to 180ºC/360ºF and air fry for 45 minutes, or until the centre of the beef reads a temperature of 52ºC/125ºF for medium rare or 57ºC/134ºF for medium. Remove the Wellington from the air fryer basket, and allow to rest for 5 minutes before slicing.

Top tips

Slice your mushrooms thinly too thick and your beef Wellington will end up too wide once rolled and will be too big for the air fryer.

Aim for a maximum size of 900g/2lb beef fillet so that the Wellington will fit in the air fryer.

Prosciutto or pancakes? These are both popular ingredients for layering into the Wellington to help prevent soggy pastry. We prefer to use prosciutto as it adds extra flavour to the beef.

Go diagonal If you have a smaller air fryer, you may struggle to move the Wellington. By placing it diagonally in an air fryer basket, it will be easier to get it in and out of the air fryer.

Add a non-stick layer It's important to use a paper liner or place a sheet of baking parchment under your beef Wellington to stop it sticking. Use a knife to poke air holes in the paper so that the air can still circulate and you will avoid an uncooked base. The excess paper at the sides will also give you "handles" to help you lower the Wellington in, and lift it out, of the fryer.

Flipping the beef Wellington This is important as air fryers cook from the top, so to make sure our Wellington doesn't have a soggy bottom, we turn it during cooking. Cook the bottom of the Wellington first, pastry seal up, then flip it over and then cook the top. Remember our tip for the paper liner above? Well that also makes it easier to flip.

Don't overcook your beef! Remember that beef Wellington will continue cooking for a little while once it comes out of the air fryer. Aim for 52°C/125°F for medium rare, and it will finish at 55°C/131°F once it is done resting.

Start small When we first made a beef Wellington, we were very aware of the cost involved. Therefore, we made two mini Wellingtons out of **two 170g/6oz fillet steaks**. It was the perfect portion for the two of us. To do this, sear the steaks and assemble as in the recipe, but decrease the other main ingredient quantities and use: **85g/3oz mushrooms**; **300g/10½oz pastry**; **60g/2oz pâté**; **60g/2oz prosciutto**. Cook, pastry seal up, at 180°C/360°F for 10 minutes, then flip it over and cook at 200°C/400°F for another 10 minutes.

Adjust for your air fryer size If you have a smaller air fryer, you could also make a smaller Wellington with a **675g/1½lb beef fillet**. When going smaller, reduce the main ingredients to the following: **85g/3oz mushrooms**; **250g/9oz pastry**; **60g/2oz pâté**; **60g/2oz prosciutto**. Cook at 180°C/360°F for 15 minutes, then flip it over and cook for another 18 minutes for medium rare or another 22 minutes for medium. A Wellington this size will still feed four people (rather than six from a big one), so it is still a great choice.

Dual air fryer if you have a dual air fryer, you are likely to have a problem fitting a full-sized Wellington into the air fryer drawer. If this is you, we recommend doing two smaller ones, as mentioned above.

everyday meatloaf wellington

While a classic beef wellington is great for special occasions, the everyday version is a meatloaf wellington, using minced beef instead. This tastes so good, I could eat it every Sunday, forever!

SERVES **6**
HERO **BASKET**
PREP **15 MINUTES**
COOK TIME **35 MINUTES**
CALORIES **608**

1 small white onion
450g/1lb minced/ground beef
1 tsp garlic purée
2 tsp tomato purée/paste
1 tsp dried parsley
2 tsp sweet paprika
2 tsp mixed herbs/Italian seasoning
1 tbsp Worcestershire sauce
1 large egg, plus 1 beaten egg, to glaze
28g/1oz/½ cup panko breadcrumbs
Plain/all-purpose flour, for dusting
½ x 500g/1lb 2oz block of puff pastry
85g/3oz/1 cup grated Cheddar cheese
Salt and black pepper

FOR THE KETCHUP GLAZE
1 tbsp tomato ketchup
1 tbsp barbecue sauce
1 tsp smoked paprika
1 tsp garlic purée

01 Peel and finely dice the onion. Tip it into a bowl and add the beef, garlic and tomato purées, parsley, sweet paprika, mixed herbs, Worcestershire sauce, egg and breadcrumbs. Season well with salt and pepper, and mix well with your hands until well combined, then shape the mixture into a loaf shape.

02 Flour a clean worktop and your rolling pin, and roll out the puff pastry to a large rectangle measuring about 33 × 23cm/13 × 9 inches. In a ramekin, combine all the glaze ingredients, then brush an even layer over the pastry using a pastry brush, leaving a 1cm/½ inch border around the edge for the egg wash.

03 Sprinkle the cheese over the glaze to create an even layer, then place the meatloaf in the centre.

04 Brush a layer of egg wash over the border around the edge of the pastry. Carefully roll the pastry over the meatloaf to create a tight parcel, tucking in the pastry at the sides as you go.

05 Poke holes in a paper air fryer liner so that the air can circulate and place the liner in the air fryer basket. Carefully place the Wellington in the air fryer basket over the paper liner, with the seal side upwards (and best side down – you'll flip it later), and brush the top with egg wash. Cook at 180°C/360°F for 15 minutes.

06 Use the sides of the paper liner as handles to help you lift the Wellington out of the air fryer onto a worktop. Carefully roll it over, so it's now the right way up and place back onto the paper liner. Cut small slits in the pastry along the top of the Wellington to let the steam escape so that the pastry won't go soggy. Use the liner again to carefully place the Wellington back into the air fryer basket and brush the top and sides with egg wash. Cook for a further 20 minutes, or until the centre of the beef reads an internal temperature of 70°C/160°F or above. Remove the meatloaf Wellington from the air fryer basket and allow to rest for 5 minutes before slicing.

Feeding one but love Wellington? Follow the meatloaf Wellington recipe above, but instead of making a loaf, form the meat mixture into 10 meatballs. Roll out the pastry, add the glaze and the cheese, then cut the pastry into 10 equal-sized squares. Place a meatball in each square and fold it into a neat parcel, then brush with the egg wash. You can then cook yourself three for dinner, and freeze the remainder for later. Air fry at 180°C/360°F for 20 minutes.

Use low-fat meat This is important when making a meatloaf Wellington. We used a 5 per cent fat minced/ground beef; go higher and the fat will cause the pastry of the wellington to go soggy.

joan's quick pork bites & veggies

I met a lovely lady called Joan as I gave a demo on how to cook my rainbow vegetables in the air fryer (see page 26). She mentioned she had just purchased a pork steak and asked if she could add it to the mix. This pork bite and veggie recipe is dedicated to you, Joan, and is also perfect for one.

....

SERVES **1**
HERO **BASKET/DUAL**
PREP **5 MINUTES**
COOK TIME **15 MINUTES**
CALORIES **452**

....

1 × 225g/8oz pork steak
A pinch of dried thyme
1 Rainbow Veggie Bag (see
   page 26)
Salt and black pepper

01 Chop your pork steak into bite-sized chunks and put them in a mixing bowl. Add the thyme, season with salt and pepper, and mix with your hands to coat.

02 Add your veggie bag to the bowl and mix well with your hands until the veggies and pork bites are mixed together.

03 Tip the pork and veggies into the air fryer basket/drawer. Set the temperature to 180°C/360°F and cook for 15 minutes, or until the pork reaches an internal temperature of 70°C/160°F or above and the butternut squash is fork tender.

Swap pork for chicken We also love buying pre-diced chicken breast and using that instead of pork. Just add 5 minutes to the cooking time.

20-minute weeknight sausage dinner (two ways)

Sausages are one of our favourite foods to prepare in the air fryer. They cook quickly, are cheap compared to most other meats, and are perfect for easy weeknight dinners. Here are two of our favourite recipes.

sausage & rainbow peppers

Sausages are cooked with different coloured peppers, red onion and some simple seasonings all at the same time.

SERVES **2**
HERO **BASKET/DUAL**
PREP **8 MINUTES**
COOK TIME **20 MINUTES**
CALORIES **667**

3 (bell) peppers/capsicums (in any colour combination of red, yellow, green)
1 red onion
6 thick sausages
2 tsp extra virgin olive oil
2 tsp dried oregano
Salt and black pepper

01 Deseed the peppers and chop them into strips, and peel and finely slice the red onion. Put the peppers and onion in a bowl and add the sausages, olive oil and oregano. Season with salt and pepper, and mix well with your hands.

02 Tip the sausages, onion and peppers into the air fryer basket/drawer. Set the temperature to 180ºC/360ºF and cook for 15 minutes. Give the basket or drawer a good shake, then cook for a further 5 minutes until the sausages are brown to your liking and the peppers and onion are nice and crispy.

Summer sausage traybake If you love a sausage traybake, ring the changes with this summery version. Peel **2 sweet potatoes** and dice them into 2cm/¾ inch cubes. Chop **1 courgette/zucchini** and **1 red (bell) pepper** the same size. Put the chopped veg into a bowl and add **6 thick sausages, 1 tablespoon extra virgin olive oil, 2 teaspoons garlic purée, 2 teaspoons dried oregano** and **1 teaspoon dried thyme**. Season well with **salt and black pepper** and mix well with your hands. Cook at 180ºC/360ºF for 13 minutes, then add **170g/6oz cherry tomatoes**, halved, give everything a shake, and cook for another 7 minutes or until the sweet potatoes are fork tender and the sausages are brown to your liking.

the ultimate doner kebab fakeaway

When we lived in Portugal, Kyle and I truly missed our doner kebabs, so we recreated them for the air fryer.

....

SERVES **4**
HERO **BASKET/DUAL**
PREP **10 MINUTES**
COOK TIME **50 MINUTES, PLUS RESTING**
CALORIES **691**

....

900g/2lb lean minced/ground lamb
Saskia's Flatbread (see page 196)

FOR THE DONER SEASONING
1 tbsp dried oregano
1 tbsp dried thyme
1 tbsp mixed herbs/Italian seasoning
1 tbsp dried coriander/cilantro
1 tbsp ground cumin
1 tbsp sweet paprika
1 tsp onion powder
1 tsp cayenne pepper
Salt and black pepper

FOR THE GARLIC SAUCE
240ml (8fl oz/1 cup) fat-free Greek yoghurt
1 garlic clove, minced
1 tsp dried parsley

FOR THE KEBAB SALAD
2 medium tomatoes
¼ medium cucumber
¼ medium white onion
A small chunk of red cabbage

01 Combine all the ingredients for the doner kebab seasoning in a bowl, add a good amount of salt and pepper, and mix well.

02 Add the lamb to the bowl with the seasoning and mix well with your hands. Form the spiced lamb mixture into a log the shape of a meatloaf.

03 Lay a large sheet of foil (big enough to wrap the kebab in) out on your worktop. Place the doner loaf in the centre and wrap it tightly with the foil. Place the wrapped doner kebab in the air fryer basket/drawer, with the foil seal up. Set the temperature to 160ºC/320ºF and cook for 25 minutes.

04 When the air fryer beeps, open up the foil carefully, to create a layer of foil in the bottom of the air fryer which will hold the juices but expose the meat. Increase the temperature to 180ºC/360ºF and air fry for a further 25 minutes, or until the lamb is fully cooked.

05 In the meantime, mix the garlic sauce ingredients together in a small serving bowl, then put to one side.

06 For the salad, slice the tomatoes and cucumber and finely slice the onion. Shred the cabbage and sprinkle them over a platter.

07 When the doner meat is cooked, allow it to rest for 30 minutes, then it will slice better, like true doner meat. Whilst you are waiting, you can prepare and air fry the flatbreads.

08 Once rested, slice your doner into thin slices or use a vegetable peeler for a perfect slice. Serve the doner meat with salad, warm flatbread and garlic sauce.

Batch prepare your seasoning Combining all the elements for the seasoning takes a while, so we make it in large batches – usually five times the mix above – and store it in a plastic container so that it's ready for future kebabs.

Got a dual air fryer? Then for the ultimate fakeaway, cook the doner kebab in one drawer and the French fries (see page 154) in the other.

dom's burger in a bowl

In the summer, when we have some minced/ground beef in the fridge, I will smile at Dom and ask for a burger in a bowl for lunch. This recipe uses the typical ingredients of a burger, minus the bread. Instead, it is served like a salad and is delicious and perfect for the summer diet.

....

SERVES **2**
HERO **BASKET/DUAL**
PREP **10 MINUTES**
COOK TIME **20 MINUTES**
CALORIES **418**

....

FOR THE BURGERS
225g/½lb lean minced/ground beef
1 tsp mustard powder
2 tsp dried basil
1 tsp lightest cream cheese
1 tbsp grated Cheddar cheese
Salt and black pepper

FOR THE BURGER SALAD
1 small lettuce (such as baby gem)
1 large tomato
¼ medium white onion
10 gherkin/pickle slices

FOR THE BURGER SAUCE
1 tsp tomato ketchup
2 tbsp mayonnaise
2 tbsp fat-free Greek yoghurt
1 tsp gherkin/pickle juice
½ tsp English mustard
¼ tsp smoked paprika

01 Put all the ingredients for the burgers in a bowl, season with salt and pepper, and mix well with your hands. Divide the mixture into two equal portions and form each into a burger patty.

02 Put the burger patties in the air fryer basket/drawer, making sure that they are spread out and not on top of each other. Set the temperature to 180°C/360°F and cook for 20 minutes.

03 In the meantime, make the salad. Shred the lettuce and put it in a large salad dish. Slice the tomato and finely slice the onion, then scatter both over the lettuce. Finish with a layer of gherkin slices.

04 Next, make the burger sauce by combining all the sauce ingredients in a small bowl, then put to one side.

05 When the air fryer beeps, chop the burgers into bite-sized chunks and scatter them over the prepared salad. Finish the salad by drizzling the burger sauce over the top.

12-minute lamb koftas

I often buy extra minced/ground lamb from the butcher's just to make koftas. These koftas are one of the easiest kebabs to make in the air fryer and can be made with or without skewers. We usually have them as an alternative to doner kebabs (see page 106) and will serve them with the same doner kebab salad and sauce, and then enjoy them with homemade flatbreads (see page 196).

....

SERVES **2**
HERO **BASKET/DUAL**
PREP **5 MINUTES**
COOK TIME **12 MINUTES**
CALORIES **475**

....

¼ medium white onion
450g/1lb minced/ground lamb
1 tsp garlic purée
1 tbsp dried coriander/cilantro leaf
2 tsp ground cumin
¼ tsp cayenne pepper
1 tsp ground coriander
1 tsp tandoori powder
A pinch of ground cinnamon
Salt and black pepper

01 Peel and finely dice the onion. Put it in a bowl and add the lamb, garlic purée, coriander and dried spices. Season well with salt and pepper and mix everything together well.

02 Divide the mixture into six equal portions and shape them into koftas – which are the shape of fat sausages. If using kebab skewers, thread a skewer through the length of each kofta.

03 Place as many koftas as will fit in your air fryer basket/drawers in a single layer – you may need to cook them in batches. Set the temperature to 180ºC/360ºF and cook for 12 minutes, or until cooked through.

FISH

let's air fry parmesan crusted cod

We call this our "last-minute fish for dinner" recipe as it is prepared and cooked in 20 minutes! This can be done with many different fish fillets, but we love it most with cod.

Instead of classic breading with flour, egg and breadcrumbs, you spread a sticky layer on the top of your fish, then press it upside down into the Parmesan crumb. It creates a crispy crumb on top of your fish fillets.

Top tips

Fish fillets cook fast in the air fryer Keep an eye on them until you get used to your air fryer, as it's easy to overcook them, leaving them dry.

Vary the flavours We have used our honey marinade here, but you can mix and match with any of the marinades from page 37. In the Milner house, we cook the most with the coriander and lime marinade.

Go for the underdog to save the £££ Whilst I love cod, haddock and salmon, basa, coley, and pollock are much cheaper and taste just as good.

SERVES **2**
HERO **BASKET/DUAL**
PREP **8 MINUTES**
COOK TIME **12 MINUTES**
CALORIES **280**

....

2 × 110g/3¾oz skin-on cod fish fillets
1 tsp dried parsley
½ recipe quantity of Honey and Garlic Marinade (see page 37)
1 tbsp wholegrain mustard
15g/½oz/⅓ cup panko breadcrumbs
1 tsp dried oregano
2 pinches of garlic powder
1 tbsp finely grated Parmesan cheese
Salt and black pepper

01 Pat the cod fillets dry, then season them generously with salt and pepper, and sprinkle the parsley over.

02 In a bowl, mix together the marinade and the mustard, then brush it over the cod, covering the tops and sides.

03 Combine the breadcrumbs, oregano, garlic powder and Parmesan on a dinner plate, season with salt and pepper, and use your hands to mix everything together. Place the cod fillets, skin-side up, into the crumb. Push them down firmly and move them about a bit, to create a generous coating. Then flip the cod fillets back over.

04 Place the cod fillets side by side in the air fryer basket/drawer and set the temperature to 180°C/360°F. Cook for 12 minutes, or until the cod is crispy to your liking and cooked through.

Bacon-wrapped cod fillets Instead of adding the Parmesan crumb, you can cover the fillets with bacon instead. Simply follow steps 1 and 2, then wrap each cod fillet in **3 slices of back bacon**, until fully covered – the bacon will stay in place thanks to the marinade. Air fry at 180°C/360°F for 14 minutes, or until your fish is cooked and the bacon is nice and crispy.

sofia & jorge's fish fingers, chips & beans

Sofia and Jorge love their school dinners. They have a school menu printed out and the night before school they will proudly mention what they are having. Fish Friday is their favourite and every third Friday is fish fingers/ sticks. Here is their homemade version that they always have served on their favourite blue fish themed plates.

SERVES **2**
HERO **DUAL**
PREP **10 MINUTES**
COOK TIME **23 MINUTES**
CALORIES **628**

2 medium potatoes
2 tsp extra virgin olive oil
1 tsp dried oregano
35g/1¼oz/¼ cup plain/all-purpose flour
1 tsp dried dill
1 medium egg
1 tsp lemon juice
55g/2oz/½ cup golden breadcrumbs
1 tsp dried parsley
2 × 110g/3¾oz fish fillets thawed
½ x 400g/14oz can of baked beans
Salt and black pepper

01 To prepare the chips, peel the potatoes and slice them into chunky chips/fries. Put them in a bowl with the olive oil, oregano and a generous seasoning of salt and pepper. Mix with your hands and tip them into an air fryer drawer, spreading them out so that they cook evenly. Cook the chips at 160°C/320°F for 10 minutes.

02 Meanwhile, make the fish fingers. Set up a production line. Put the flour in a shallow bowl and stir in the dill. Crack the egg into another bowl, beat it, then stir in the lemon juice. Put the breadcrumbs in a third bowl and add the parsley. Give each bowl a generous seasoning of salt and pepper, and also season the fish fillets with salt and pepper too.

03 Slice each fish fillet into two or three fish fingers. To coat, first, turn the fish fingers over in the flour to fully coat, then drench them in the egg. Finish with a double coating of the breadcrumbs. Place the fish fingers in the other drawer of the dual air fryer.

04 After the 10 minutes are up, shake the chips, then match the air fryer drawers and cook the chips and fish fingers together at 180°C/360°F for 8 minutes.

05 The fish fingers should now be cooked – just check that they are crispy enough and piping hot, then remove them from the drawer onto the kids' plates. Pour the beans into two ramekins and place them into the now empty drawer.

06 Cook the chips and beans at the same temperature for another 5 minutes, or until they are crispy and the beans are piping hot. Then serve the fish fingers, chips and beans together.

Basket fish fingers If cooking in a basket, it's a little slower because the food is not as spread out. Air fry the chips for 15 minutes at 180°C/360°F. Make some room in the basket and add the fish fingers, then air fry for another 5 minutes. Add the beans and cook everything for 5 minutes, then serve.

marinated salmon (two ways)

On page 37 we shared our marinade recipes; this is how to use them with salmon fillets to take your salmon to the next level.

hawaiian salmon with mango salsa

You will love Hawaiian salmon. Using our Hawaiian marinade and serving with a quick homemade mango salsa (which stores in the fridge perfectly) it is perfect for a summer salmon fix.

....

SERVES **2**
HERO **BASKET/DUAL**
PREP **8 MINUTES, PLUS MARINATING**
COOK TIME **14 MINUTES**
CALORIES **542**

....

2 × 110g/3¾oz salmon fillets
1 recipe quantity Hawaiian Summer marinade (see page 37)
Lemon wedges, to serve

FOR THE MANGO SALSA
2 canned pineapple rings
½ avocado
½ mango
¼ red onion
½ red chilli
1 tbsp finely chopped fresh parsley
Juice of 1 lime
1 tbsp clear honey

01 Place the salmon in a freezer bag, add the marinade and shake to get a good coating of the marinade all over the salmon. Place into the fridge to marinate for at least 2 hours.

02 Tip the salmon fillets and their marinade into a foil tray/pan and place into the air fryer basket/drawer. Set the temperature to 180ºC/360ºF and air fry for 14 minutes, or until the salmon flakes on touch.

03 While the salmon cooks, make the salsa. Chop the pineapple into chunks, peel and dice the avocado and mango, and peel and finely chop the red onion. Deseed and very finely dice the red chilli. Put everything into a mixing bowl and add the parsley, lime juice and honey. Stir everything together, then serve it with the salmon and lemon wedges for squeezing over.

Make curried salmon Place **2–4 salmon fillets** into a freezer bag with the **curry yoghurt marinade** from page 37 and shake about to mix. Marinate in the fridge for at least 2 hours, then place onto a paper liner. Place in the air fryer basket/drawer, set the temperature to 180ºC/360ºF and cook for 14 minutes, or until cooked through.

Frozen salmon If you prefer, you can prep the marinated salmon and it can go in the freezer raw for up to 3 months. Using our dual air fryer, we love to match the drawers and cook the salmon (from frozen) in one drawer and frozen rainbow veggies (see page 26) in the other drawer. They both need 160ºC/320ºF for 20 minutes.

smoked haddock with baby potatoes & green beans

Sue, our pescatarian reader, asked for fish fillets with potatoes and veg for dinner. To avoid washing up and to use everyday ingredients that can be mixed and matched, we created this recipe!

SERVES **2**
HERO **BASKET/DUAL**
PREP **8 MINUTES**
COOK TIME **25 MINUTES**
CALORIES **330**

285g/10oz baby potatoes, scrubbed
2 tbsp extra virgin olive oil
2 tsp dried parsley
140g/5oz green beans, trimmed
1 tbsp dried mixed herbs
2 × 110g/3¾oz smoked haddock fillets
A squeeze of lemon juice
Salt and black pepper
Lemon wedges and fresh dill, to serve (optional)

01 Quarter the baby potatoes and put them in a 18 × 18cm/7 × 7 inch foil tray/pan (or a size compatible with your air fryer). Season the potatoes with salt and pepper, add 1 tablespoon of the olive oil and the parsley, and mix with your hands until the potatoes are well coated.

02 Place the tray into the air fryer basket/drawer, set the temperature to 180°C/360°F and cook for 10 minutes.

03 When the air fryer beeps, shake the potatoes and add the green beans. Drizzle with the remaining olive oil and sprinkle in the dried herbs. Use a spatula to mix everything together, then air fry at the same temperature for another 5 minutes, or until the potatoes are fork tender.

04 Give the potatoes and green beans a shake. Place the haddock fillets on top of the veg and drizzle with lemon juice. Using the same temperature, cook for a further 10 minutes, or until the fish is fully cooked and flakes on touch. Transfer the haddock to dinner plates, then shake the tray to mix the potatoes and green beans in the flavoursome oil. Spoon the veg onto the plates, drizzling any oil from the bottom of the tray over the potatoes. We love to serve this with lemon wedges and a sprinkling of fresh dil.

Mix and match Thanks to fish fillets and vegetables with similar cook times it's easy to mix and match:

- Swap smoked haddock for similar-sized salmon, seabass, cod, hake or tuna fillets.
- Swap green beans for asparagus, broccolini, peppers, tomatoes or baby corn.

15-minute catfish and broccolini We mixed and matched the haddock recipe above, switching the haddock for **basa/catfish** and the veg for broccolini. Add **230g/8½oz of broccolini** to the foil tray, drizzle over **1 tablespoon olive oil**, and sprinkle with **1 teaspoon dried parsley**, then season with salt and pepper. Shake the tray to coat everything, then cook at 180°C/360°F for 5 minutes. Add the fish fillets on top, season them with salt and pepper, add **a squeeze of lemon juice** and cook for another 10 minutes until the fish is cooked through.

20-minute seafood crumble pots

These individual crumbles are perfect for smaller air fryer baskets. A crumble can also be savoury and these use frozen seafood bags, reducing the prep and are perfect for an effortless seafood starter.

SERVES **4**
HERO **BASKET/DUAL**
PREP **8 MINUTES**
COOK TIME **20 MINUTES**
CALORIES **616**

1 × 350g/12oz bag raw frozen seafood mix
Juice of 1 lemon
1 × 150g/5½oz pack of garlic and herb cream cheese (we use Boursin)
1 tbsp chopped fresh parsley
2 tsp dried thyme
2 tsp wholegrain mustard
2 tbsp grated Parmesan cheese
125g/4½oz/1 cup frozen peas
4 tbsp white wine
Salt and black pepper

FOR THE CRUMBLE TOPPING
125g/4½oz/1 cup self-raising/self-rising flour
60g/2oz/¼ cup unsalted butter, softened and diced
28g/1oz/⅓ cup porridge oats/oatmeal
2 tsp dried thyme
28g/1oz/⅓ cup grated Parmesan cheese
2 tsp English mustard powder (such as Colman's)

01 Put the frozen seafood and lemon juice into a silicone container and add a generous seasoning of salt and pepper. Unwrap the block of cream cheese and find a spot for it in the centre of the container. Transfer the container to the air fryer basket/drawer. Set the temperature to 180ºC/360ºF and cook for 10 minutes, or until the prawns/shrimp are pink and cooked through.

02 Whilst the seafood is cooking, make the crumble topping. Put all the crumble ingredients into a mixing bowl. Stir everything together, then rub the fat into the flour and oat mixture until you have a crumble topping. Season the crumble with salt and pepper.

03 Remove the container from the air fryer and add the parsley, thyme, mustard, Parmesan, frozen peas and white wine to the seafood. Mix everything together well.

04 Divide the creamy seafood filling between four ramekins (about 200ml/7fl oz/¾ cup) until three-quarters full. We find the easiest way to stop spillages is to use a ladle. Sprinkle the crumble mixture over the tops, dividing it equally among the ramekins.

05 Place the ramekins into the air fryer basket. If using the dual, you will need to divide the ramekins between the two drawers. Set the temperature to 180ºC/360ºF and cook for 10 minutes, or until golden on top and piping hot throughout.

garlic butter prawns with white wine

One of my favourite Spanish tapas dishes is prawns with garlic butter and white wine. Using frozen king prawns/shrimp it's so easy to make using the air fryer. Your guests will think you have made a great effort when you haven't.

....

SERVES **2**
HERO **BASKET/DUAL**
PREP **5 MINUTES**
COOK TIME **12 MINUTES**
CALORIES **240**

....

2 tbsp salted butter, diced
¼ medium red onion, finely chopped
4 garlic cloves, peeled and finely sliced
4 tbsp white wine
240g/8½oz frozen raw peeled king prawns/shrimp
1 tbsp finely chopped fresh parsley
A squeeze of lemon juice
Salt and black pepper

01 Put the butter, red onion, garlic and white wine in a container suitable for the air fryer basket/drawer. Set the temperature to 120°C/250°F and cook for 4 minutes.

02 Stir the melted butter and wine mixture, then add the frozen prawns. Increase the temperature to 180°C/360°F and cook for 8 minutes (or 10 minutes if your prawns are jumbo sized), or until the prawns are pink and cooked through.

03 Transfer everything to a tapas dish, including the delicious garlic wine butter, stir in parsley and season with salt and pepper. Add a squeeze of lemon juice and serve.

Serving suggestion We love to cook part-baked bread in the air fryer to dunk into the wonderful garlic and white wine cooking juices. Place four part-baked rolls into the air fryer whilst you are dishing up the prawns and air fry for 5 minutes at 180°C/360°F.

frozen prawns & avocado salsa

Inspired by a meal at a Peruvian restaurant whilst in Mexico, we air fry the king prawns/shrimp whilst we prep this quick avocado salsa. This recipe is brilliant for bringing to parties, or stuff it into a flatbread and it's perfect for when you have lots of salad items in and are looking for something different to make. This also travels well for something healthy to take to work with you.

....

SERVES **2**
HERO **BASKET/DUAL**
PREP **8 MINUTES**
COOK TIME **8 MINUTES**
CALORIES **224**

....

240g/8½oz frozen raw peeled
   king prawns/shrimp
Juice of 3 limes
¼ cucumber
½ medium avocado
175g/6oz cherry tomatoes
¼ medium red onion
a few sprigs of fresh coriander/
   cilantro
Salt and black pepper

01 Place the frozen prawns in an air fryer friendly container inside your air fryer basket/drawer. Squeeze the juice of two limes over them and season well with salt and pepper. Set the temperature to 180ºC/360ºF and cook for 8 minutes, or for 10 minutes for jumbo prawns.

02 In the meantime prepare the remaining ingredients, adding them to a salad dish as you prep them. Slice the cucumber into 1cm/½ inch thick slices, then quarter each slice, and chop the avocado into 1cm/½ inch cubes. Quarter the cherry tomatoes, and peel and finely chop the onion. Then finely chop the coriander. Stir everything together in the salad dish.

03 When the air fryer beeps, allow the prawns to cool, then place them on a chopping board and cut into 1cm/½ inch chunks. Add the prawns to the salad, season with salt and pepper and squeeze in the remaining lime. Mix with a spoon and serve.

VEGETARIAN
& VEGAN

let's air fry a warm salad

Throughout this chapter we will be sharing simple recipes for air-fried veggies. But what about combining some of your vegetables into a warm salad? We make warm salads in autumn and winter, and for enjoying the last of the root vegetables in spring before summer arrives.

best of autumn maple salad with toasted lentils

SERVES **2**
HERO **BASKET/DUAL**
PREP **12 MINUTES**
COOK TIME **33 MINUTES**
CALORIES **507**

225g/8oz butternut squash
  (prepared weight, see method)
225g/8oz sweet potatoes
2 tbsp extra virgin olive oil
½ tsp sweet paprika
1 tsp pumpkin spice
225g/8oz Brussels sprouts
2 tsp maple syrup
2 tsp balsamic vinegar
½ x 400g/14oz can brown lentils,
  drained
60g/2oz rocket/arugula leaves
Salt and black pepper

FOR THE SALAD DRESSING
1 tbsp balsamic vinegar
1 tbsp maple syrup
1 tbsp extra virgin olive oil
1 garlic clove, minced

This is our vegan autumn salad that we make when our favourite fall foods are in season. It's loaded with butternut squash, sweet potatoes and Brussels sprouts, all flavoured with a maple–balsamic glaze. Mix with rocket and toasted lentils for the wow factor.

01 Peel the butternut squash and sweet potato, and dice into 2cm/¾ inch cubes. Put them in a mixing bowl with 1 tablespoon of the olive oil, the sweet paprika, and half the pumpkin spice. Mix well with your hands. Tip into the air fryer basket/drawer and spread out so that they cook evenly. Set the temperature to 180°C/360°F and cook for 10 minutes.

02 In the meantime, prepare the sprouts. Slice them in half and put in a bowl with 2 teaspoons of the olive oil, and the maple syrup and balsamic vinegar. Season generously with salt and pepper, then mix with your hands. When the air fryer beeps, add the sprouts and shake the basket/drawer to allow the sprouts to mix well with the butternut squash and sweet potatoes. Air fry at the same temperature for a further 15 minutes.

03 While the air fryer is busy, prepare the lentils in the same bowl as you did the sprouts. Add the lentils, the remaining 1 teaspoon of olive oil and the remaining pumpkin spice. Season with salt and pepper and mix with your hands, then put to one side.

04 To prepare the salad dressing, put all the dressing ingredients in a jug, season with salt and pepper and mix with a fork, then set side.

05 When the air fryer beeps, toss the rocket leaves into the roasted autumn vegetables and divide between two serving plates. Add the lentils to the air fryer basket/drawer and air fry at 200°C/400°F for 8 minutes, or until toasted. Sprinkle the toasted lentils over the salad and drizzle with the salad dressing before serving.

creamy root vegetable soup

When we arrived in Finland to visit Santa last Christmas, it was -8°C/-17°F and we were tired from travelling. The hotel served us the most amazing warm and comforting root vegetable soup and I vowed there and then to recreate it in the air fryer. I have added coconut milk and ginger to make it creamy and for some winter spice.

....

SERVES **4**
HERO **DUAL**
PREP **8 MINUTES**
COOK TIME **30 MINUTES**
CALORIES **549**

....

2 medium carrots
1 large sweet potato (about 450g/1lb)
2 medium parsnips
1 tbsp extra virgin olive oil, plus an optional drizzle for the top
1 tbsp mixed herbs/Italian seasoning
½ tbsp dried rosemary
½ tbsp dried thyme
1 × 150g/5½oz pack garlic and herb cream cheese (we use Boursin)
1 × 400g/14oz can full-fat coconut milk
1½ tbsp ground ginger
Salt and black pepper

01 Peel the carrots, sweet potato and parsnips, and dice them all into 2cm/¾ inch cubes. Put them in a bowl with the olive oil, mixed herbs, rosemary and thyme. Season with salt and pepper, and mix well with your hands.

02 Tip the root vegetables into the air fryer basket, or spread out between two dual drawers. Set the temperature to 160°C/320°F and cook for 15 minutes.

03 When the air fryer beeps, shake the air fryer basket/drawers. Take the top foil off your cheese and place the cheese in the centre of the air fryer, on top of the vegetables. Increase the temperature to 180°C/360°F and cook for a further 10 minutes.

04 Add a can of coconut milk to a blender, then refill the coconut can and scrape the edges, getting every last bit of coconut that is stuck to the sides. Add the roast vegetables, reserving a few of the vegetables for serving over your soup. Scoop the cheese out of the rest of the foil and add it to the blender along with the ground ginger, and pulse until you have a smooth soup. Taste and adjust the seasoning with salt and pepper. The soup will now be warm, but not piping hot. If you would like it hotter, pour it into an air fryer container (or into the drawer of the dual without the crisper plate) and air fry at 180°C/360°F for another 4–5 minutes.

05 Divide the soup among four bowls, top each one with a few of the reserved roasted vegetables and finish with an optional extra drizzle of olive oil.

Freezer friendly This soup freezes well. Pour into your favourite freezer container and freeze for up to 3 months, or it will keep for up to 3 days in the fridge.

sweet potato & chickpea curry

The process of making an air fryer curry is a simple one. You air fry your dry ingredients first (your sweet potato and chickpeas), before creating your curry sauce. We like to serve it with our homemade garlic and coriander naan bread (see box below).

....

SERVES **4**
HERO **BASKET/DUAL**
PREP **8 MINUTES**
COOK TIME **35 MINUTES**
CALORIES **807**

....

2 medium sweet potatoes
1 tbsp extra virgin olive oil
1 tsp dried coriander/cilantro leaf
¼ tsp mild curry powder
¼ tsp ground turmeric
1¼ tsp garam masala
1 × 400g/14oz can chickpeas, drained
Salt and black pepper
Garlic and Coriander Naans (see opposite), to serve

FOR THE CURRY SAUCE

4 frozen spinach blocks, thawed
1 × 400ml/14oz can coconut milk
240ml/8fl oz/1 cup passata
4 tsp tikka paste
2 tsp ginger purée
2 tsp dried coriander/cilantro leaf
1 tsp ground cumin

01 Peel the sweet potatoes and dice them into 2cm/¾ inch cubes. Put them in a mixing bowl and add the olive oil, coriander leaf, curry powder, turmeric and ¼ teaspoon of the garam masala. Season generously with salt and pepper, mix with your hands and tip into the air fryer basket/drawer.

02 Set the temperature to 180ºC/360ºF and cook for 20 minutes. Add the chickpeas to the air fryer with the sweet potatoes and sprinkle the remaining garam masala over the top. Mix well with a spatula for an even coating, then cook at the same temperature for another 5 minutes.

03 Put all the curry sauce ingredients in a silicone container that fits into your air fryer and mix well with a spatula. When the air fryer beeps, transfer the sweet potatoes and chickpeas to the container and stir in.

04 Place the silicone container into the air fryer basket and air fry at the same temperature for another 10 minutes. Your curry will now be piping hot and ready for serving, along with some naan.

Dual curry Instead of a silicone container, when it's time to mix the curry sauce with the other ingredients, remove the crisp plate and cook directly in the bottom of the drawer. If serving with naan bread, have a curry in one drawer and naan in the other.

Garlic and coriander naan This naan bread is made with our air fryer flatbread dough and is delicious served with our sweet potato and chickpea curry above. Simply make a portion of **Saskia's two-ingredient yoghurt dough** on page 196, swapping the plain/all-purpose flour for self-raising/self-rising flour. As you knead the dough, incorporate **2 teaspoons garlic purée** and **1 tablespoon dried coriander/cilantro leaf**. Cook the naan at 180ºC/360ºF for 4 minutes. While the breads are cooking, in a bowl combine **2 tablespoons olive oil, 1 teaspoon dried coriander leaf** (or use **1 tablespoon finely chopped fresh coriander**) and **1 teaspoon garlic purée**. Brush the naans with the flavoured oil and cook for another 4 minutes at the same temperature.

vegan falafel subs

We love falafel in the air fryer. Mainly because they are quick cooking, but also because of how crispy they go without needing extra oil. Take them to the next level by serving in a vegan sub.

SERVES **4**
HERO **BASKET/DUAL**
PREP **10 MINUTES**
COOK TIME **25 MINUTES**
CALORIES **456**

2 vegan part-baked baguettes
115g/4oz vegan cheese, grated

FOR THE FALAFEL BALLS
1 × 400g/14oz can chickpeas
1 tsp extra virgin olive oil
2 tsp ground cumin
1 red (bell) pepper/capsicum
¼ red onion
1 tsp ground coriander
1 tsp smoked paprika
1 tsp garlic purée
½ tsp ground ginger
¼ tsp cayenne pepper
1 tbsp dried parsley
Plain/all-purpose flour, for your
  hands

FOR THE TOMATO SAUCE
6 tbsp passata
1 tbsp tomato purée/paste
2 tsp garlic purée
2 tsp dried basil
2 tsp dried oregano
Salt and black pepper

01 Drain the chickpeas and add them to a mixing bowl. Add the olive oil and half the cumin, and mix with your hands. Tip into the air fryer basket/drawer and cook for 2 minutes at 180ºC/360ºF. This will help to dry the excess moisture from the chickpeas and make them easier to bind. Transfer your chickpeas to a blender/food processor.

02 Slice the pepper into 2cm/¾ inch squares and put them in the same bowl you used for the chickpeas. Season with salt and pepper and the remaining cumin and mix with your hands, then tip into the air fryer. Cook for 5 minutes at 200ºC/400ºF.

03 When the air fryer beeps, tip the pepper into the blender with the chickpeas and add the remaining falafel ingredients. Blitz until everything comes together into a thick paste.

04 Form the blended mixture into 12 falafel balls, flouring your hands as you need to stop them sticking. Place the balls into the air fryer basket, or spread between two drawers if using a dual. Cook at 180ºC/360ºF for 12 minutes, or until the falafels are nice and golden, and piping hot.

05 In the meantime, in a small bowl, mix together the tomato sauce ingredients, then set aside.

06 When the air fryer beeps, slice open the part baked baguettes and slice in half creating two smaller baguettes from each one. Spread a layer of the tomato sauce over each, then add three falafel balls to each one and coat with more tomato sauce. Divide the grated cheese between the subs and place them in the air fryer. I can fit all four in a standard sized air fryer, or two in each dual drawer. Air fry at 160ºC/320ºF for 6 minutes, until the cheese is melted and the sauce is piping hot.

Vegan cheese We have found that some vegan cheeses struggle to melt quickly in the air fryer. You can either melt the cheese fast in the microwave (20 seconds full power) or leave the subs in the air fryer to stay warm for an extra 5 minutes, as the heat will help with the melting.

Part-baked bread We love using part-baked bread in the air fryer and it averages half the cook time of the oven instructions on the packaging. You can use baguettes and slice them in half like we have done above, or use small crusty rolls.

baked macaroni cheese

This macaroni cheese is a brilliant concept. Every ingredient is loaded into a foil container in one go – no adding ingredients bit by bit – making it very fast to prep. It's similar to baked mac and cheese, and thanks to using cream cheese there is no separate cheese sauce to make.

SERVES **4**
HERO **BASKET**
PREP **5 MINUTES**
COOK TIME **40 MINUTES**
CALORIES **781**

250g/9oz dried macaroni pasta
375g/13oz/4 cups grated mature/sharp Cheddar cheese
600ml/21fl oz/2½ cups whole/full-fat milk
2 tsp garlic purée
2 tsp English mustard
1 tbsp dried oregano
1 × 150g/5½oz pack garlic and herb cream cheese (we use Boursin)
Salt and black pepper

FOR THE CRISPY TOPPING
1 tbsp panko breadcrumbs
1 tbsp grated Parmesan cheese
1 tsp dried basil

01 Put all the ingredients except the cream cheese into a 18cm/7 inch square foil tray/pan and stir together, then make a space in the middle and place the cream cheese block in it.

02 Place the foil container carefully into the air fryer basket. Set the temperature to 180ºC/360ºF and cook for 35 minutes, stirring every 9 minutes to avoid clumping together. (We usually set the timer for 9 minutes at a time to remind ourselves to stir!) As you stir, the cream cheese will be mixed in and you will have a creamy macaroni cheese. At first it will not resemble mac and cheese, but have patience and when the liquid is fully absorbed by the pasta in the last few minutes of the cooking time, it will come together.

03 Once the time is up, do a taste test (the best job!), double checking the pasta is soft and it's nice and cheesy, and adding more salt and pepper if needed.

04 Combine the ingredients for the crispy topping in a small bowl. Sprinkle it over the top of the mac and cheese and cook for a few more minutes at 200ºC/400ºF, or until light golden, then serve.

Dual mac and cheese You can choose a foil container that fits the dual, or make the macaroni cheese directly in the drawer, removing the crisper plate first. If using the bottom, add an extra 10 minutes at 180ºC/360ºF.

Dishes We have made this mac and cheese in a casserole dish (as photographed), in a foil container, direct in the bottom of our dual, and in silicone. You can keep the same cook times and just go with whichever container you prefer.

easy-prep vegetarian enchiladas

These vegetable and taco bean enchiladas are so good that I will make two batches: one for dinner tonight, the other for the freezer (see tip).

SERVES **2**
HERO **BASKET/DUAL**
PREP **10 MINUTES**
COOK TIME **30 MINUTES**
CALORIES **599**

1 × 300g/10½oz jar of tomato salsa
4 small tortilla wraps
Extra virgin olive oil spray
115g/4oz/1¼ cups grated Cheddar cheese

FOR THE FILLING
½ red (bell) pepper/capsicum
¼ aubergine/eggplant
¼ medium red onion
½ tbsp extra virgin olive oil
2 tsp ground cumin
2 tsp ground coriander
½ tsp dried oregano
½ tsp smoked paprika
½ × 400g/14oz can mixed taco beans in tomato sauce
½ tbsp sour cream
40g/1½oz/½ cup grated Cheddar cheese
1 tbsp jalapeño slices from a jar
35g/1¼oz/¼ cup sweetcorn
Salt and black pepper

TO SERVE (ALL OPTIONAL)
Sliced avocado
Fresh coriander/cilantro
Sour cream

01 Chop the pepper and the aubergine into 2cm/¾ inch cubes. Slice the red onion into 1cm/½ inch thick slices. Put the chopped vegetables in a bowl and add the olive oil, ½ teaspoon of the cumin, ½ teaspoon of the coriander, the oregano and paprika, and a generous seasoning of salt and pepper. Mix well with your hands, then tip into the air fryer basket/drawer. Air fry at 180°C/360°F for 15 minutes or until the peppers have a barbecue-style grilled look.

02 Whilst the veggies are cooking, put all the remaining filling ingredients in a mixing bowl and add half the jar of salsa. When the veggies are cooked, add them to the bowl and stir.

03 Divide the filling evenly among the tortilla wraps. Roll each one up tightly, tucking in the top and bottom as you roll, like you're preparing a burrito. Place the enchiladas, side by side, in an 18cm/7 inch square foil tray/pan – or a ceramic dish, paper liner or silicone container will also work well. Push them close together in the tray to keep them in place.

04 Spray the tops of the enchiladas with olive oil to help them crisp up, then place the tray in the air fryer basket. Air fry at 180°C/360°F for 8 minutes, or until they are crisp and not soggy at all.

05 Spoon over enough of the remaining salsa to cover the wraps, then sprinkle the Cheddar over the top. Continue to air fry at 160°C/320°F for 7 minutes, or until the salsa is piping hot and the cheese has melted.

06 Serve the enchiladas with your choice of toppings, such as avocado, coriander and/or sour cream.

Dual enchiladas You can choose a foil container that fits the dual, or we prefer to use the bottom of the dual from step 3.

Make a double batch We'll often make a double batch of the filling, then fill and roll eight tortilla wraps rather than four. That way we can place four in the freezer, ready to pull out and cook when needed.

Non-stick Add a dessertspoon of salsa to the bottom of your container. It will stop the wraps from sticking and make them easier to remove once cooked.

Bowl leftovers If you have spare filling mix, you can combine it with the salsa for the topping. We found when we scraped the bowl we had about 2 teaspoons leftover to use up.

creamed spinach & butternut squash tart

As a former vegetarian, I always hated only having the choice of a nut roast or mushrooms when eating out for Christmas lunch. I also know other vegetarian's whose pet peeve is cheese being in everything. This tart is nut free, mushroom free and cheese free. You will also love our hack for cooking the squash and blind baking the pie crust at the same time.

SERVES **6**
HERO **BASKET**
PREP **10 MINUTES**
COOK TIME **35 MINUTES**
CALORIES **374**

180g/6¼oz/1⅓ cups plain/all-purpose flour, plus extra for dusting
90g/3¼oz/6 tbsp salted butter
225g/8oz butternut squash (prepared weight)
2 tsp extra virgin olive oil
3 tsp dried parsley
¼ red onion
200g/7oz frozen spinach (about 5 blocks), thawed
240ml/8½oz/1 cup sour cream
1 large egg, beaten
1 tbsp garlic purée
2 tsp dried oregano
A handful of fresh basil leaves, shredded
Salt and black pepper

01 Put the flour in a mixing bowl and add the butter, cubing it as you add it. Rub the fat into the flour using your fingertips until the mixture resembles breadcrumbs. Gradually add about 3 tablespoons water and mix with your hands until everything comes together and you have a soft pastry dough. Lightly flour your kitchen worktop and a rolling pin, and roll out the pastry until 3mm/⅛in thick and large enough to line a 20cm/8 inch loose-bottomed pie tin. Lift the pastry with the rolling pin and use it to line the tin.

02 Peel the butternut squash and chop it into 1cm/½ inch cubes. Put them in a mixing bowl with the olive oil and 1 teaspoon of the parsley, season with salt and pepper and mix well with your hands. Arrange the cubes in a single layer over the pastry. Place the pie tin in the air fryer, set the temperature to 180ºC/360ºF and cook for 15 minutes.

03 In the meantime, make your creamed spinach filling. Peel and finely slice the red onion and put it in a mixing bowl. Squeeze any excess moisture out of the spinach, then add that to the bowl, along with the sour cream, beaten egg, garlic purée, oregano, finely chopped basil and the remaining parsley. Mix everything together well.

04 When the air fryer beeps, carefully remove the squash from the pastry case and put to one side. Spoon the creamed spinach into the pastry case, then scatter the roasted butternut squash over the top of the tart.

05 Air fry the tart at 180ºC/360ºF for 20 minutes, or until the pie crust is golden, the creamed spinach is heated through and your butternut squash is getting crispy. Leave the tart in the air fryer to cool for 5 minutes, then remove the tin from the air fryer. Slice into 6 wedges and serve warm.

Dual mini tarts Instead of using one large pie tin, you can also make the tart in two 10cm/4 inch pie tins. Divide the ingredients between the two and cook one in each drawer. Because they are smaller, the final cook time is just 15 minutes.

moroccan lentil-loaded sweet potato steaks

Sweet potato steaks are delicious and a fun vegan food that are perfect when sweet potatoes are in season. A gigantic sweet potato will make two large steaks, which we pair with delicious Moroccan-spiced lentils.

SERVES **2**
HERO **BASKET/DUAL**
PREP **8 MINUTES**
COOK TIME **42 MINUTES**
CALORIES **798**

1 gigantic sweet potato
  (800g–1kg/1¾–2¼lb)
Extra virgin olive oil spray
1 tsp ground cumin
1 tsp smoked paprika
Salt and black pepper
Vegan sour cream or thick
  yoghurt, to serve

FOR THE LOADED LENTILS
1 recipe quantity Moroccan
  Marinade (see page 37)
1 × 400g/14oz can chopped
  tomatoes
1 × 400g/14oz can of brown
  lentils, drained
1 small white onion, finely diced
2 tsp ground cumin
2 tbsp finely chopped
  coriander/cilantro

01 Peel the sweet potato, then stand it up and slice through it to create two large slices, each about 3.5cm/1½ inches thick. Trim to make two 225g/8oz sweet potato steaks that measure approximately 12cm/4½ inches in length and 8cm/3¼ inches wide. (Or if your sweet potato is smaller you can make 175g/6oz steaks – see tip below.)

02 Spray the steaks with olive oil and sprinkle with the cumin and a good seasoning of salt and pepper. Place them in the air fryer basket, side by side, or put one in each dual drawer. Set the temperature to 160ºC/320ºF and cook for 30 minutes. Turn the sweet potato steaks over with tongs and spray with olive oil again. Add a sprinkle of smoked paprika and cook at 200ºC/400ºF for a further 4 minutes.

03 In the meantime, put the Moroccan marinade in a silicone container. Add the tomatoes, brown lentils, onion, cumin, coriander and a generous seasoning of salt and pepper. Mix well and set aside.

04 When the air fryer beeps, remove the steaks and add the container with the lentils to the air fryer (or put them directly in the drawer without the crisper plate, if using a dual). Cook at 180ºC/360ºF for 8 minutes, or until piping hot. Pour the Moroccan lentils over the sweet potato steaks, and serve with a dollop of vegan sour cream or yoghurt.

Smaller steaks If you're cooking smaller 175g/6oz sweet potato steaks, reduce the cook time to 20 minutes at 160ºC/320ºF, with the same 4 minutes at 200ºC/400ºF.

Trimmings We love to use the sweet potato trimmings to make some crisps/chips, then transform them into our sweet potato nachos from page 150.

Swap steaks for baked potatoes Make our lentil recipe above, but instead serve it with the baked sweet potatoes from page 153.

Vegetarian lentil wraps Any leftover lentils can be used to fill wraps for a quick lunch. Spread a wrap with **cream cheese**, then add **3 heaped tablespoons of Moroccan lentils**, sprinkle with **28g/1oz/ ⅓ cup grated mozzarella cheese** and wrap it tightly. Brush the top the with **beaten egg**, then air fry at 180ºC/360ºF for 6 minutes. Flip the wrap over, brush the top with egg, and air fry at the same temperature for a further 2 minutes.

famous feta (three ways)

Blocks of feta cheese are like magic in the air fryer, because they cook fast and work with a lot of different recipes. They have become famous across social media, especially combined with cherry tomatoes. Here are three of our favourite feta recipes, including the famous pasta sauce.

greek baked feta

If you have ever visited Greece, the chances are you have enjoyed baked feta. This recipe takes just 8 minutes to cook and shouts out simplicity.

SERVES **2**
HERO **BASKET/DUAL**
PREP **5 MINUTES**
COOK TIME **8 MINUTES**
CALORIES **325**

1 × 200g/7oz block of feta cheese
225g/8oz cherry tomatoes
2 tsp extra virgin olive oil
2 tsp dried oregano
1 tsp dried thyme
Crusty bread, to serve

01 Put the block of feta into an air fryer-safe dish or silicone air fryer container. Scatter the tomatoes into the dish around the feta, then drizzle with the olive oil and sprinkle with the dried herbs.

02 Place the silicone container in the air fryer basket/drawer. Set the temperature to 180ºC/360ºF and cook for 8 minutes, or until lightly baked. Serve with crusty bread.

Feta pasta sauce If you cook the feta and cherry tomatoes for longer and stir, it's like a creamy tomato sauce and is perfect for pasta, casseroles and many other similar recipes. To do this, simply follow the recipe opposite but cook for 15 minutes instead of 8 minutes. Tip the contents of the container into a blender or food processor, add **1 teaspoon minced garlic** and **2 tablespoons fat-free Greek yoghurt** and blend for a smooth creamy sauce. Or, for a Tuscan-style sauce, just stir rather than blending and the tomatoes will have a similar texture to sun-dried tomatoes.

Feta cheese & chive dip Make the pasta sauce above and leave it in the fridge to chill for at least 2 hours and it will thicken like a Mediterranean dip. You can then flavour your dip and serve it with your favourite bread or crackers. We like to add the following to ours: **1 finely chopped small red onion, 85g/3oz/1 cup grated mature/sharp Cheddar cheese, 2 tablespoons finely chopped fresh chives** and **1 tablespoon dried basil**. If you'd like your dip warm, air fry at 160ºC/320ºF for 6 minutes, or until warmed through.

ravioli bites

We first fell in love with these ravioli bites 8 years ago. The idea is simple: fresh, prepared ravioli is breaded and air fried. They are perfect for an easy appetiser.

....

SERVES **2**
HERO **BASKET/DUAL**
PREP **8 MINUTES**
COOK TIME **6 MINUTES**
CALORIES **583**

....

1 large egg
35g/1¼oz/¼ cup plain flour/
  all-purpose flour
28g/1oz/½ cup panko
  breadcrumbs
2 tbsp grated Parmesan cheese
2 tsp dried oregano
A pinch of garlic powder
175g/6oz fresh prepared
  vegetarian ravioli
Salt and black pepper
Feta Cheese and Chive Dip
  (see page 143), to serve
  (optional)

01 Crack the egg into a bowl, then beat with a fork. Put the flour in another shallow bowl. Put the breadcrumbs in a third bowl, add the Parmesan, oregano, garlic powder and a generous seasoning of salt and pepper, and stir with a fork. Your bowls are now ready for breading.

02 Coat the ravioli first in the flour, then dredge in the egg and finish with a thorough coating of the breadcrumbs.

03 Gently place the breaded ravioli into the air fryer basket/drawer spreading them out, so that they cook evenly. Set the temperature to 200ºC/400ºF and cook for 6 minutes, or until crispy, then serve with the dip, if making.

avocado wedges

SERVES **2**
HERO **BASKET/DUAL**
PREP **8 MINUTES**
COOK TIME **8 MINUTES**
CALORIES **412**

2 medium avocados, not too ripe
1 large egg
35g/1¼oz/¼ cup plain flour/
    all-purpose flour
28g/1oz/½ cup panko
    breadcrumbs
2 tsp taco seasoning
A pinch of garlic powder
Salt and black pepper

Avocados are sliced into wedges and breaded with panko crumbs flavoured with taco seasoning – perfect for using up your avocados.

01 Peel the avocados, remove the stones and slice into wedges. We usually get 8 wedges per avocado.

02 Crack the egg into a bowl, then beat with a fork. Put the flour in another shallow bowl. Put the breadcrumbs in a third bowl, add the taco seasoning, garlic powder and a generous seasoning of salt and pepper, and stir with a fork. Your bowls are now ready for breading.

03 Gently turn the avocado wedges over in the flour to coat, then dredge in the egg and finish with a thorough coating of the breadcrumbs.

04 Gently place the breaded avocado wedges into the air fryer basket/drawer spreading them out so that they cook evenly. Set the temperature to 200°C/400°F and cook for 8 minutes, or until crispy.

salt & pepper tofu

SERVES **2**
HERO **BASKET /DUAL**
PREP **8 MINUTES**
COOK TIME **16 MINUTES**
CALORIES **205**

½ red (bell) pepper/capsicum
½ green (bell) pepper/capsicum
½ medium red onion
1 red chilli
250g/9oz tofu, pressed
1 tbsp extra virgin olive oil
4 tsp Chinese 5-spice powder
Salt and black pepper

Move aside salt and pepper chips/fries. This is how to make the Chinese takeaway classic using tofu.

01 Slice the peppers into strips, and slice the red onion. Slice the red chilli, discarding the seeds (or keep them in if you like the heat). Slice the tofu into thick strips, like chunky chips/fries.

02 Put everything in a bowl and add the olive oil and 5-spice powder. Season with salt and pepper and mix well with your hands, but be gentle, as you don't want the tofu to break.

03 Transfer everything to the air fryer basket/drawer and set the temperature to 200°C/400°F. Cook for 16 minutes, or until the peppers are tender and the tofu has got a crisp to it.

Press your tofu This will help it crisp up. Place the tofu block on a plate between two clean tea towels/dish towels. Place something heavy (such as a heavy pan) on top and let it sit for an hour to squeeze out any excess moisture before using in recipes.

POTATOES

let's air fry crisps

Air fryers make light work of making your own crisps (or potato chips, as you might call them). Potatoes are sliced super thin on a mandolin, then tossed in extra virgin olive oil. Season them with your favourite dried seasonings, then after a quick mix with your hands, the crisps/chips are ready for the air fryer.

They are perfect for a quick snack, or why not use them to make our sweet potato nachos (see page 150)

SERVES **2**
HERO **BASKET/DUAL**
PREP **10 MINUTES**
COOK TIME **13 MINUTES**
CALORIES **531**

....

4 medium white potatoes
3 tbsp extra virgin olive oil
2 tsp mixed herbs/Italian
   seasoning
A pinch of garlic powder
Salt and black pepper

01 Preheat the air fryer to 200°C/400°F. Peel the potatoes, then using a mandolin on a 2mm/$\frac{1}{16}$ inch setting, slice the potatoes into very thin discs. Discard any ends that are not a uniform circle shape.

02 Put the potato slices in a bowl and add the olive oil, herbs and garlic powder. Season with salt and pepper, and mix well with your hands.

03 Arrange the sliced potatoes in the air fryer basket or spread out over two dual drawers, making sure that they are in a single layer (you will need to cook them in batches). Keep the temperature at 200°C/400°F and cook for 7 minutes. Use tongs to flip the crisps over and cook at the same temperature for another 6 minutes, or until crispy and light golden.

Sweet potato crisps We prefer to use white potatoes because it's quicker to get them nice and crispy in the air fryer, and also easier to get white potatoes in a uniform shape. If you would rather do sweet potatoes, follow the recipe above but use **425g/15oz sweet potatoes** and slice them across the width so that you get nice round crisps and not long floppy oval ones. Add an extra 1 minute of cooking time on each side, and if you feel some are still not crispy enough, add a couple of extra minutes, but remove the cooked ones first.

Top tips

Use what you have You can use white, red or sweet potatoes as they all have a similar cook time. Avoid small potatoes because the size of crisp will be too small.

Don't scrimp on the oil Compared to other air fryer potato recipes, you need more olive oil for crisps, to create the perfect crispy texture.

Keep a close eye on them As they are so thin, they can burn quickly, so we keep an eye on them and give them a check after 10 minutes, and if they need to be crispier (they may still feel soggy on touch), give them a little longer.

Choose your flavour Try our mixed herb crisps (opposite), or add 2 teaspoons of your favourite dried seasonings. This can be a combination of seasoning or just one. Why not try:

- Salt and black pepper
- Smoked paprika and ground cumin
- Curry powder
- Chinese 5-spice powder
- Dried basil
- Cajun seasoning
- Fajita seasoning
- Shawarma seasoning

Love apples and pears? Using your mandolin, cut thin slices of apple and/or pear to make fruit crisps instead. Cook them at the same time and temperature as the potato crisps. Instead of the delicious flavour options above, you can dust them with pumpkin spice, ground cinnamon, or a mixture of the two. They make a fantastic snack and are great for putting in your kids lunch boxes.

sweet potato nachos

I love nachos and the more loaded they are, the better. I want sour cream, guacamole, avocado, melted cheese and plenty of beans. We use a loose-based pan, because it makes transferring the nachos to a serving plate easier.

SERVES **2**
HERO **BASKET**
PREP **10 MINUTES**
COOK TIME **8 MINUTES**
CALORIES **978**

1 recipe quantity Sweet Potato Crisps (see page 148)
1 x can 400g/14oz taco beans in tomato sauce
1 tsp ground coriander
1 tsp garlic powder
1 tsp sweet paprika
140g/5oz/1 cup frozen sweetcorn
170g/6oz/2 scant cups grated mature/sharp Cheddar cheese
6 pickled jalapeños, sliced, plus extra to sprinkle
Salt and black pepper

TO SERVE (ALL OPTIONAL)
2 tbsp sour cream
2 tbsp guacamole
Fresh coriander/cilantro

01 Create a layer of sweet potato crisps/chips in the bottom of a 20cm/8 inch dish.

02 Drain the mixed taco beans, and put them in a mixing bowl. Add the ground coriander, garlic powder, sweet paprika and frozen sweetcorn, then season with salt and pepper and mix well.

03 Sprinkle half the grated cheese over the sweet potato crisps, then add the taco bean mixture, followed by the remaining cheese. Finish by sprinkling over the sliced jalapeños. As you layer up, don't take the toppings right to the edges – you will then have some crisps/chips that are bare at the edges and can be grabbed easily when the nachos are cooked.

04 Place the dish in the air fryer basket. Set the temperature to 180ºC/360ºF and cook for 8 minutes, or until the beans are heated through and the cheese is melted.

05 Remove the dish from the air fryer with oven gloves as it will be hot. Use a spatula to get underneath and remove the nachos from the base, transferring them to a serving platter. We like to serve them with sour cream and guacamole, and sprinkled with fresh coriander leaves and more jalapeños, but it's up to you!

Dual nachos When making this in the dual air fryer, we swap the dish for two rectangular ones that perfectly fitted the dual drawers, then divide the ingredients equally between them.

Lighten the load If you have a night of nachos in front of the TV planned and you prefer to be free of washing up, you can make these in a foil tray instead.

baked sweet potatoes

I love cooking sweet potatoes in the air fryer. But one question that comes up time and time again is, 'How long do sweet potatoes take?" Or 'Why are my potatoes still hard and yours aren't?' The easiest way to avoid sweet potatoes with uncooked (or overcooked) centres is to refer to our chart with the cooking times of various sizes of sweet potatoes, which you can refer back to when you need it.

....

SERVES **2**
HERO **BASKET/DUAL**
PREP **3 MINUTES**
COOK TIME **45 MINUTES**
CALORIES **337**

....

Extra virgin olive oil spray
2 large sweet potatoes
  (approximately 450g/1lb
  each), scrubbed
Salt and black pepper
Your choice of fillings, to serve

01 Spray a dinner plate with olive oil and season it generously with salt and pepper.

02 Roll the sweet potatoes in the olive oil and seasoning until they are well coated.

03 Place the sweet potatoes in a single layer in the air fryer basket/drawer. Set the temperature to 180ºC/360ºF and cook for 45 minutes, or until the sweet potatoes are fork tender.

04 To serve, place a sweet potato on a dinner plate, slice in half and load it up with your favourite toppings.

Sweet potato cooking times This is our guide for how to adapt cooking times for different sizes of potatoes (arranged by size in the photo, left). Whether you are cooking one potato or four, the cook time doesn't change.

- 150g/5½oz (small) – 20 minutes
- 300g/10½oz (medium) – 25 minutes
- 450g/1lb (large) – 45 minutes
- 550g/1¼lb (extra large) – 55 minutes
- 700g/1lb 9oz (extra extra large) – 60 minutes
- 900g/2lb (gigantic) – 75 minutes

simply the best skin-on seasoned french fries

In the Milner house, we just love to recreate fast-food-style fries in the air fryer. We love the way they are cooked in their skin, with just the right amount of seasoning. Because they are thin cut, they cook quicker and, thanks to the skin and seasoning, they are so wonderfully crispy.

....

SERVES **2**
HERO **BASKET/DUAL**
PREP **5 MINUTES**
COOK TIME **20 MINUTES**
CALORIES **349**

....

3 medium potatoes
4 tsp extra virgin olive oil
2 tsp dried oregano
Salt and black pepper

01 Scrub the potatoes, then using a knife or a potato chipper, cut the potatoes into French fries.

02 Put the fries in a bowl and add the olive oil and oregano. Season with salt and pepper, and mix well with your hands.

03 Tip the potatoes into the air fryer basket/drawer and spread them out so that they cook evenly. Set the temperature to 160°C/320°F and cook for 15 minutes. Shake the basket, then increase the temperature to 200°C/400°F and cook for a further 5 minutes, or until crispy to your liking.

Go sweet potato If you're like Jorge and prefer sweet potatoes, you can swap like for like and keep the same time and temperature.

garlic parmesan hasselback potatoes

We love baby potatoes in the air fryer. Cooked whole, they go so crispy and are fork tender in a third of the time of large potatoes. One way to take them to the next level is to prepare hasselback potatoes, which we make taste even better with garlic and Parmesan.

SERVES **2**
HERO **BASKET/DUAL**
PREP **10 MINUTES**
COOK TIME **25 MINUTES**
CALORIES **377**

675g/1½lb baby potatoes
1 tbsp extra virgin olive oil
1 tbsp dried oregano
1 tbsp garlic purée
28g/1oz/½ cup grated
  Parmesan cheese
Salt and black pepper

01 To create hasselback potatoes, slice each potato at 2–3mm/¹⁄₁₆th inch intervals, only taking the knife three-quarters of the way down so that the slices are still joined at the base and the potato is still in one piece.

02 Put the sliced potatoes in a mixing bowl and add the olive oil and oregano. Season with salt and pepper, and mix well with your hands. Add the garlic purée and mix again – the garlic will create a sticky coating on the potatoes. Add the Parmesan to the bowl and mix a final time to create a Parmesan coating over the potatoes.

03 Carefully tip the potatoes into the air fryer basket/drawer and spread them out so that they cook evenly. Set the temperature to 180ºC/360ºF and cook for 25 minutes, or until the hasselback potatoes are crispy and fork tender.

Cutting tip When slicing these, it's easy to go a little hard on the knife and cut all the way through the potato. To stop this happening, insert a metal skewer lengthways into the potato, about 5mm/¼ inch up from the base. The knife will hit the skewer each time you cut down and stop you cutting all the way through.

baby potatoes (three ways)

If I could choose one favourite potato, it would be baby. They are so versatile – from slicing to cubing to quartering, or just keeping them whole. Also, because the skin tastes so good, you have no peeling to do, which speeds up your prep time. Below you will find our three favourite ways to cook them – from Spanish potatoes, to a hearty breakfast version, to spiced Bombay potatoes to serve with your curry.

spanish chorizo & pepper potatoes

We love these Spanish potatoes. Quartered baby potatoes are loaded up with red peppers, onion and chorizo, and seasoned with paprika.

SERVES **4**
HERO **BASKET/DUAL**
PREP **10 MINUTES**
COOK TIME **25 MINUTES**
CALORIES **290**

....

675g/1½lb baby potatoes
1 red (bell) pepper/capsicum
1 small red onion
2 tbsp extra virgin olive oil
1 tsp smoked paprika
1 tsp dried oregano
1 tsp dried coriander/cilantro leaf
1 tsp garlic purée
85g/3oz chorizo, diced
Salt and black pepper
Oregano leaves, to garnish (optional)

01 Scrub the baby potatoes, then cut them into quarters. Slice the red pepper and onion into a similar shape. Put the potatoes, peppers and onion in a mixing bowl and add all the remaining ingredients apart from the chorizo. Season with salt and pepper, and mix well with your hands.

02 Tip the potatoes into the air fryer basket/drawer and spread them out so that they cook evenly. Set the temperature to 180ºC/360ºF and cook for 20 minutes.

03 When the air fryer beeps, shake the potatoes, then add the chorizo to the air fryer basket over the potatoes. Increase the temperature to 200ºC/400ºF and cook for a further 5 minutes, or until the potatoes are crispy and fork tender, and the chorizo is nice and crispy too.

04 Serve the potatoes hot – as they are, or they are lovely sprinkled with oregano leaves.

Breakfast potatoes These are similar to Spanish potatoes and carry the same cook time and temperature. Swap the chorizo for the same quantity of **bacon bits**, then swap out the paprika, coriander and garlic for **1 tablespoon dried parsley** and increase to **1 tablespoon dried oregano**.

Make-ahead Bombay potatoes When we are having a curry night (see page 191), we prep the Bombay potatoes ahead and then cook the potatoes at the same time as the curry to save time and make dinner even easier. Simply prep the same amount of potatoes, as in the recipe above. Put them in a mixing bowl and, instead of the additions above, add **1 tablespoon extra virgin olive oil**, **1 teaspoon ground coriander**, **1 teaspoon garam masala**, **1 teaspoon mild curry powder**, **1 teaspoon garlic purée** and **1 teaspoon ginger purée**, and season with **salt and black pepper**. You can now continue to cook them at the same time and temperature as above.

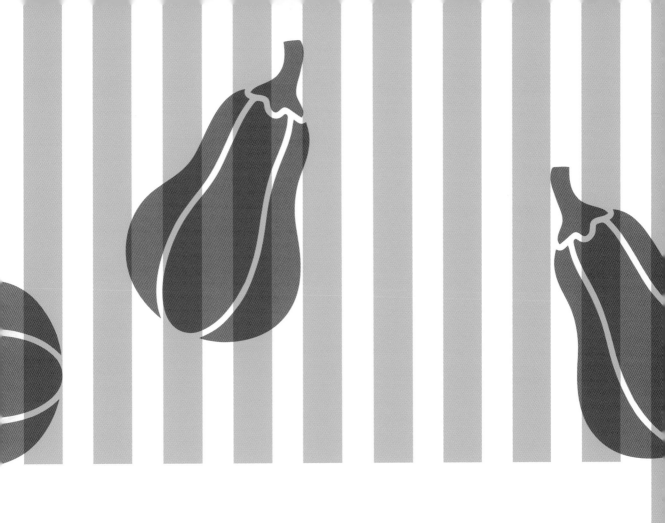

VEGETABLES

quick-cook sunday vegetables

This is a brilliant and effortless way of cooking your favourite Sunday dinner vegetables in the air fryer. Potatoes, parsnips, carrots and Brussels sprouts come together in one air fryer basket, ready for serving alongside your favourite Sunday roast.

SERVES **4**
HERO **BASKET/DUAL**
PREP **10 MINUTES**
COOK TIME **30 MINUTES**
CALORIES **262**

3 medium white potatoes
4 large carrots
1 large parsnip
2 tbsp extra virgin olive oil
1 tsp dried rosemary
1 tsp dried thyme
225g/8oz Brussels sprouts
1 tbsp balsamic vinegar
1 tbsp dried parsley
salt and black pepper

01 Scrub and peel the potatoes, carrots and parsnip, then dice them into 2cm/¾ inch cubes. Put the vegetables in a bowl and add the olive oil, rosemary and thyme. Add a generous seasoning of salt and pepper, and mix well with your hands.

02 Tip the veg into the air fryer basket/drawer and spread out so that they cook evenly. Set the temperature to 160ºC/320ºF and cook for 10 minutes.

03 In the meantime, prepare the sprouts. Clean and chop them in half, then put them in the bowl. Drizzle with balsamic vinegar, add the parsley, season with salt and pepper and mix with your hands. Once the root vegetables have been cooking for 10 minutes, tip the prepared sprouts into the air fryer and use a spatula to mix everything together. Continue air frying for another 10 minutes.

04 When the air fryer beeps, shake the air fryer basket/drawer, increase the temperature to 180ºC/360ºF and cook for a further 10 minutes, or until the root vegetables are fork tender.

simply the easiest cauliflower cheese

We have some simple tricks to make this creamy cauliflower cheese even easier. Combining frozen cauliflower with a leftover veggie cheese sauce, this is perfect for Sunday dinners, Christmas or just a simple dinner side dish.

SERVES **4**
HERO **BASKET/DUAL**
PREP **5 MINUTES**
COOK TIME **25 MINUTES**
CALORIES **767**

675g/1½lb frozen cauliflower florets
1 tsp dried oregano
1 tsp dried mixed herbs/Italian seasoning
1 recipe quantity Bits and Bobs Cheese Sauce (see page 33)
85g/3oz/1 cup grated mature/sharp Cheddar cheese, for sprinkling
Salt and black pepper

01 Place the frozen cauliflower florets into the air fryer basket/drawer and spread out so that they cook evenly. Set the temperature to 180°C/360°F and cook for 15 minutes.

02 When the air fryer beeps, transfer the just-cooked cauliflower to a silicone pan or casserole dish with handles. (If using a dual, you can use two smaller dishes and cook one in each drawer.) Sprinkle the herbs over the cauliflower and season with salt and pepper. Pour over the cheese sauce and sprinkle grated cheese over the top.

03 Place the dish into the air fryer basket/drawer, set the temperature to 180°C/360°F and air fry for 10 minutes, or until the cheese sauce is heated through and the cheese on top has melted.

Why do we use frozen cauliflower? Frozen cauliflower cooks quickly in the air fryer, doesn't go hard like fresh and, of course, saves you on prep time.

everyday air fryer veggies

If you are looking for simple everyday veggies in the air fryer, you will love these. Each recipe needs only five ingredients or less, making them perfect for weeknights, and choices include leeks, spring greens, aubergine and cauliflower.

crispy leeks

Do you ever have one leek leftover and wonder what to do with it? Let me introduce you to crispy leeks; shredded leek, simple seasoning and olive oil work like a dream. Enjoy it as a side, or sprinkle it over soups.

SERVES **2**
HERO **BASKET/DUAL**
PREP **5 MINUTES**
COOK TIME **14 MINUTES**
CALORIES **34**

1 large leek
Extra virgin olive oil spray
1 tsp dried oregano
Salt and black pepper

01 Slice the leek in half, then slice each half into 1cm/½ inch slices, to create a shredded look. Using a sieve, wash the leek under cold water, then pat dry with kitchen towel/paper towel.

02 Tip the shredded leek into the air fryer basket/drawer and spread it out so that it cooks evenly. Set the temperature to 160°C/320°F and cook for 8 minutes.

03 Shake the shredded leeks, generously spray with olive oil, sprinkle with oregano, and season with salt and pepper. Air fry at 200°C/400°F for a further 6 minutes, or until crispy to your liking.

shredded spring greens

I look forward to when spring greens are in my weekly vegetable box. You can quickly shred them (or buy them sliced) and toss in oil and seasoning and they taste so good when air fried.

SERVES **2**
HERO **BASKET/DUAL**
PREP **5 MINUTES**
COOK TIME **10 MINUTES**
CALORIES **104**

225g/8oz sliced spring greens
1 tbsp extra virgin olive oil
1 tbsp dried parsley
Salt and black pepper

01 Place the sliced spring greens in a bowl and add the olive oil and the parsley. Season generously with salt and pepper and mix with your hands until they are evenly coated.

02 Tip the spring greens into the air fryer basket/drawer and spread them out so that they cook evenly.

03 Set the temperature to 180°C/360°F and cook for 10 minutes, or until the edges are starting to crisp and are cooked to your liking.

parmesan-coated aubergine slices

My aunt, when visiting from the USA, would take me shopping for 'eggplant'. It wasn't until I was a grown up that I realised eggplant was what us Brits call 'aubergine'. They are still a favourite and are delicious sliced and air fried with Parmesan.

SERVES **2**
HERO **BASKET/DUAL**
PREP **5 MINUTES**
COOK TIME **13 MINUTES**
(PER BATCH)
CALORIES **107**

1 large aubergine/eggplant
Extra virgin olive oil spray
28g/1oz/⅓ cup grated Parmesan cheese
Salt and black pepper

01 Slice the aubergine into 1cm/½ inch thick slices. Arrange the aubergine slices in your air fryer basket/drawers, adding as many as you can fit in a single layer – we usually need to cook our aubergine in three batches.

02 Spray the tops with the olive oil spray and season with salt and pepper. Set the temperature to 180ºC/360ºF and cook for 10 minutes, or until the aubergine is crispy and fork tender.

03 When the air fryer beeps, sprinkle the tops of the aubergine slices with Parmesan and air fry at the same temperature for 3 minutes to melt the cheese. If necessary, repeat the process to cook the remaining aubergine.

cauliflower steaks

This is crispy cauliflower with less prep. Simply slice a cauliflower into thick steak-like slices and you're ready to air fry.

SERVES **4**
HERO **BASKET/DUAL**
PREP **5 MINUTES**
COOK TIME **18 MINUTES**
CALORIES **61**

1 large cauliflower
Extra virgin olive oil spray
2 tsp taco seasoning
Salt and black pepper

01 Place the cauliflower on a chopping board, stalk side down, and slice the cauliflower into 2.5cm/1 inch thick slices. You can usually get four good sized steaks from a large cauliflower – they will each need a bit of the core to help hold them together, so any slices from the ends that fall apart can be used for another recipe.

02 Place the cauliflower steaks in the air fryer basket/drawer and spread them out so that they cook evenly. Spray the tops with the olive oil spray and sprinkle evenly with the taco seasoning and salt and pepper.

03 Set the temperature to 180ºC/360ºF and cook for 12 minutes. When the air fryer beeps, adjust the temperature to 160ºC/320ºF and air fry for a further 6 minutes, or until fork tender and crispy to your liking.

jalapeño poppers

If there is a party food you must air fry, it is jalapeño poppers. They are quick to prepare, taste delicious and travel well for taking to a gathering.

....

MAKES **32**
HERO **BASKET/DUAL**
PREP **8 MINUTES**
COOK TIME **12 MINUTES**
CALORIES **43**

....

1 tbsp salted butter
16 jalapeño chillies
165g/5¾oz/¾ cup cream cheese
115g/4oz/1¼ cups grated mature/sharp Cheddar cheese
1 tsp garlic purée
1 spring onion/scallion, thinly sliced
4 tsp dried coriander/cilantro leaf
28g/1oz/½ cup panko breadcrumbs
Salt and black pepper

01 Put the butter in a ramekin and place the ramekin in the air fryer. Set the temperature to 120ºC/250ºF and air fry for 4 minutes, or until the butter is melted.

02 Slice the jalapeños lengthways and remove the seeds. Discard the seeds and wash your hands; there is nothing worse than touching your face, especially your eyes, after touching the spicy peppers.

03 Put the cream cheese, Cheddar cheese, garlic purée, spring onion, and half the dried coriander into a mixing bowl. Season with salt and pepper and mix well with a spoon. Spoon the mixture into the jalapeños.

04 In another bowl, combine the breadcrumbs, melted butter and the remaining coriander, and mix with a fork. Grab one filled jalapeño at a time and push it, cream cheese down, into the breadcrumbs. The breading will stick to the cheese filling to create a crust. Repeat for all the jalapeño halves until they all have a crust.

05 Carefully place the jalapeños into the air fryer basket/drawer, set the temperature to 180ºC/360ºF and cook for 8 minutes, or until crispy to your liking.

Bacon-wrapped jalapeño poppers I often get asked for party food ideas for gluten-free guests, or for those that eat low-carb. These bacon wrapped poppers are ideal. Simply skip the breaded crust and wrap each popper in **half a slice of streaky bacon** instead. Give them an extra 2 minutes of cooking time to really crisp up the bacon.

seriously crispy corn

SERVES **2**
HERO **DUAL/BASKET**
PREP **2 MINUTES**
COOK TIME **12 MINUTES**
CALORIES **140**

280g/10oz/2 cups frozen
  sweetcorn
1 tsp extra virgin olive oil
1 heaped tsp smoked paprika
Salt and black pepper

With nut allergies in the house, we're always looking for a delicious snack that has a similarly nutty, satisfying texture. This crispy corn is it! You can mix it up with different dried seasonings and it has a similar texture to crisps/chips.

01 Put the frozen sweetcorn in a mixing bowl, add the olive oil and paprika, and season generously with salt and pepper. Mix well with your hands until the sweetcorn is well seasoned.

02 Tip the sweetcorn into the air fryer basket/drawer. Set the temperature to 180°C/360°F and cook for 8 minutes. Shake the sweetcorn to help it crisp up evenly, then increase the temperature to 200°C/400°F and cook for a further 4 minutes, or until crispy to your liking. A fun thing to do to check it's cooked is to shake the air fryer basket/drawer – when it's ready you will hear the crunchy corn rattle in the air fryer.

Crispy peas You can also make crispy peas in the same way, keeping the same cook time and temperature. Or why not mix and match and make crispy corn and peas?

three-ingredient creamed corn

SERVES **2**
HERO **BASKET/DUAL**
PREP **2 MINUTES**
COOK TIME **12 MINUTES**
CALORIES **387**

1 × 150g/5½oz pack of garlic
  and herb cream cheese (we
  use Boursin)
210g/7½oz/1½ cups frozen
  sweetcorn
1 tsp dried basil

If there is a food that Kyle would have me cooking for him 24/7, it would be creamed corn. He loves the creamy sauce and the warm corn. But there are often lots of ingredients. This easy cheat's version has just three ingredients!

01 Unwrap the cream cheese and place it in the centre of a silicone container, then place the container in the air fryer basket/drawer. Set the temperature to 180°C/360°F and cook for 5 minutes.

02 When the air fryer beeps, add the frozen sweetcorn around the block of cheese. Then sprinkle the basil over the cheese and sweetcorn. Air fry at the same temperature for a further 7 minutes.

03 When the air fryer beeps, the cheese will have a really soft texture. Stir with a silicone spatula until you have a creamy corn, before serving.

avoid-the-waste broccoli ends

SERVES **1**
HERO **BASKET/DUAL**
PREP **6 MINUTES**
COOK TIME **12 MINUTES**
CALORIES **108**

Stems from 2 large broccoli
  heads
extra virgin olive oil spray
1 tsp dried coriander/cilantro
  leaf
Salt and black pepper

Try our broccoli ends and you'll be surprised by how something so simple – made with something you usually throw out – can taste so good. Made from the chunky stems of broccoli heads and sliced like vegetable fries, they will become your new air fryer go-to.

01 Peel the broccoli stems, then slice them into sticks the size of French fries. Put them in a bowl, spray with olive oil and sprinkle with coriander. Season generously with salt and pepper, and mix well with your hands.

02 Tip into the air fryer basket/drawer and spread out so that they cook evenly. Set the temperature to 180ºC/360ºF and cook for 10 minutes, or until fork tender.

03 Spray the fries again with olive oil, then increase the temperature to 200ºC/400ºF and cook for a further 2 minutes, or until starting to get crispy.

Save those ends For a bigger batch, each time you use a broccoli head, slice off the stem and freeze it in a freezer bag. Once you have six, you will be able to make a good-sized portion. If you're making a big batch, cook for 15 minutes instead of 10.

12-minute broccolini

SERVES **2**
HERO **BASKET/DUAL**
PREP **2 MINUTES**
COOK TIME **12 MINUTES**
CALORIES **63**

200g/7oz long-stem broccoli/
  broccolini
extra virgin olive oil spray
2 pinches of dried coriander/
  cilantro leaf
Salt and black pepper

Long-stem broccoli is much easier to air fry than regular broccoli florets. This is because the leafy tops of regular florets get overcooked whilst the stem is still not fork tender. Thanks to the shape and size of broccolini, it cooks much more evenly. If the stems of your broccolini are quite chunky, halve them lengthways so that they cook more evenly. (Pictured on page 173)

01 Place the broccolini into the air fryer basket/drawer and spread out so that it cooks evenly. Spray with the olive oil and sprinkle with coriander, then season generously with salt and pepper.

02 Set the temperature to 160ºC/320ºF and cook for 12 minutes, or until the leafy tops are crispy and the stem is fork tender.

oregano-crusted beetroot wedges

I had to live in Portugal to appreciate how delicious beetroot is. Over there, it sits proudly next to the broccoli and carrots, and is most loved by the locals when it's roasted and added to salad. Adding extra oregano creates a crispy crust. If you have not cooked raw beetroot before, this is a fun alternative to potato wedges that you must try.

....

SERVES **4**
HERO **BASKET/DUAL**
PREP **8 MINUTES**
COOK TIME **25 MINUTES**
CALORIES **84**

....

6 medium raw beetroots/
  beets
1 tbsp extra virgin olive oil
1 tbsp white wine vinegar
4 tsp dried oregano
Salt and black pepper

01 Peel and slice your beetroot into wedges – we usually get eight wedges from a medium beetroot. If they are out of season and a bit smaller, quartering them usually works well.

02 Put the beetroot wedges in a bowl, add the olive oil, vinegar and oregano, and season generously with salt and pepper. Mix well with your hands.

03 Tip the beetroot wedges into the air fryer basket/drawer and shake the air fryer basket/drawer to naturally spread them out. Set the temperature to 180°C/360°F and cook for 25 minutes, or until the beetroot is fork tender and the oregano is crispy. If your wedges are large, we recommend adding another 5 minutes cooking time at the same temperature.

'But beetroot is messy' This is the most common response I receive whenever I say I love peeling, chopping and air frying beetroot. Yes, your chopping board and bowl will be a little red after prep, and your hands will go pinker, but after two washes, they will all be perfect again. Although I recommend avoiding a white board and bowl, as it will show up a lot more on these.

butternut squash for everything

Butternut squash is so versatile. It can be transformed from simple roasted squash to a purée, a mash, or a curry sauce with some simple hacks.

SERVES **2**
HERO **BASKET/DUAL**
PREP **5 MINUTES**
COOK TIME **40 MINUTES**
CALORIES **171**

1 medium whole butternut
   squash
Extra virgin olive oil spray
¼ tsp dried parsley
Salt and black pepper

01 Cut a slice off the base of the butternut squash to make a flat, stable surface, then stand it up and slice through it lengthways to create two halves. Use a spoon to scoop out the seeds.

02 Spray the flesh of the butternut squash with olive oil, then sprinkle with parsley and season generously with salt and pepper.

03 Place the butternut squash halves in the air fryer basket, or if using a dual, place a squash half in each drawer. Set the temperature to 180°C/360°F and cook for 40 minutes, or until the butternut flesh is fork tender.

Butternut squash mash Follow the roasted butternut squash recipe, but wrap **2 peeled garlic cloves** in foil and cook in the air fryer with the squash. Scoop the cooked flesh out of the squash and add it to a bowl with the soft cooked garlic and a generous sprinkling of **salt and pepper**. Mash with a potato masher before serving.

Butternut squash purée To transform into a purée, air fry the squash for another 10 minutes at the same temperature until it is super soft. Remove the squash flesh from the skin and tip into a bowl. Use a hand blender to mix until you have a creamy purée. The purée is perfect for baby food, to use as a base for a creamy sauce, or for adding hidden veggies to your kids' meals.

Butternut squash curry sauce Make as the purée recipe above, but wrap **3 peeled garlic cloves** in foil and cook in the air fryer with the squash. Then after puréeing add **1 tablespoon thick Greek yoghurt**, **1 teaspoon ground cumin** and **1 teaspoon garam masala** along with a sprinkling of **salt and pepper**. Stir well.

Freezer cubes Once cool, my favourite option is to spoon the curry sauce into large ice cube trays (we use ones that are 240ml/8½fl oz/1 cup volume) and place in the freezer. Once frozen, move the ice cubes to a freezer bag, then you can just grab one (or more) when you need it. Defrost in a silicone pan in the air fryer at 160°C/320°F for 5 minutes. You can use it as a base for air fryer curry and it's delicious. (See our Chicken Tikka Masala on page 191.)

crispy courgette fries

After the jalapeño poppers on page 168, the best vegetable for breading is courgette. Because these were popular in the US first, I always find myself saying 'zucchini fries'.

We air fry the courgette first, which reduces its watery texture then bread it and crisp up in the air fryer.

....

SERVES **2**
HERO **BASKET/DUAL**
PREP **8 MINUTES**
COOK TIME **20 MINUTES**
CALORIES **229**

....

1 medium courgette/zucchini
2 tsp dried oregano
35g/1¼oz/¼ cup plain flour/
   all-purpose flour
1 large egg
45g/1½oz/1 cup panko
   breadcrumbs
1 tsp dried thyme
1 tsp dried basil
Extra virgin olive oil spray
Salt and black pepper
Burger sauce (see page 108),
   for dunking (optional)

01 Slice the courgette into fries, put them in a bowl and add the oregano and a generous seasoning of salt and pepper. Mix to evenly coat, then tip them into the air fryer basket/drawer. Set the temperature to 200°C/400°F and cook for 12 minutes.

02 In the meantime, put the flour into a shallow bowl. Crack the egg into another bowl and beat with the fork. Put the breadcrumbs into a final bowl, add the thyme and basil, season generously with salt and pepper, and mix with a fork.

03 When the air fryer beeps, toss the courgette/zucchini fries, a few at a time, first in the flour, then drench them in the egg, then roll them in the breadcrumbs to thoroughly coat.

04 Place the courgette/zucchini fries back into the air fryer basket/drawer and spread out so that they cook evenly. If using a dual, you can spread them between the two drawers. Spray the tops with olive oil. Set the temperature to 200°C/400°F and cook for 8 minutes, or until crispy to your liking. We like to serve them with burger sauce for dunking!

7 DAYS OF DINNERS

make-ahead monday: simple leftovers pie

After a roast dinner on a Sunday, Dom will do the dishes while I prepare the Monday pie, a leftover tradition we have had for more than 15 years. We love having the Monday pie prepared in the fridge, so that the next day's dinner just needs reheating.

If you've not experienced the delights of Monday pie, the filling is made from leftover roast dinner meat, baked beans, passata and bacon, and can also include other vegetables. It is topped with sliced potatoes.

....

SERVES **4**
HERO **BASKET/DUAL**
PREP **10 MINUTES**
COOK TIME **50 MINUTES**
CALORIES **419**

....

1 white onion
4 back bacon slices/rashers
Extra virgin olive oil spray
225g/8oz leftover roast lamb (see page 192, or see tip)
1 × 400g/14oz can baked beans
400g/14oz/1½ cups passata
4 tbsp gravy
1 tbsp Worcestershire sauce
1 tbsp dried thyme
1 tsp sweet paprika
½ x 540g/1lb 3oz can whole potatoes
½ tbsp extra virgin olive oil
½ tsp dried parsley
Salt and black pepper

01 Peel and slice the onion, then slice the bacon into 1cm/½ inch squares. Put the onion and bacon into your air fryer basket/drawer, spreading them out so that they cook evenly. Spray with olive oil spray, set the temperature to 180ºC/360ºF and air fry for 10 minutes, or until the bacon is crispy.

02 In the meantime, chop the lamb into 1cm/½ inch chunks. Add the lamb to a mixing bowl, add the baked beans, passata, gravy, Worcestershire sauce, thyme and paprika, and stir everything together.

03 When the air fryer beeps, stir the crispy bacon and onion into the pie filling, season with salt and pepper, and mix well.

04 Slice the canned potatoes into 5mm/¼ inch thick slices and put them in a bowl. Add the olive oil and parsley and season well with salt and pepper. Mix well with your hands until they are evenly coated.

05 Find a casserole dish that fits your air fryer and tip the filling into it. (If using the dual, I will spread the mixture between two small casserole dishes or enamel pie tins.) Place the potato slices over the top of the pie filling, overlapping and making sure there are no gaps.

06 Carefully place the dish into the air fryer basket/drawer, set the temperature to 180ºC/360ºF and cook for 40 minutes, or until the pie is warmed through and the potatoes are golden and crispy.

Tip You can use any leftover meat for this pie. We used leftover lamb from the Sunday roast lamb dinner, but pork, chicken, beef and gammon/ham also work well.

Freezer friendly To make ahead for the freezer, make this pie filling, leaving off the potatoes, then freeze in a foil tray/pan. The night before air frying, transfer from the freezer to fridge to defrost, then add the sliced potatoes just before air frying.

hectic tuesday:
make-ahead moussaka

We call Tuesday 'Hectic Tuesday' because, like most parents, it's the night when your kids need to be everywhere: Jorge is at cooking class, 90 minutes later Sofia is at cooking class, then an hour later Kyle is at football practice. This make-ahead moussaka can be made the day before and simply reheated in those few minutes you have available.

······································

SERVES **4**
HERO **DUAL**
PREP **15 MINUTES**
COOK TIME **27 MINUTES**
CALORIES **1145**

······································

1 large aubergine/eggplant
Extra virgin olive oil spray
675g/1½lb minced/ground lamb
1 small onion, peeled and diced
1 tbsp dried oregano
250g/9oz/1 cup passata
1 tbsp mixed herbs/Italian seasoning
2 tsp dried thyme
2 tsp dried basil
2 tsp garlic purée
2 tsp tomato purée/paste
1 recipe quantity Bits and Bobs Sauce for
  Everything (see page 33)
85g/3oz/1 cup grated mature/sharp Cheddar
  cheese
28g/1oz/½ cup grated Parmesan
Salt and black pepper
1 recipe quantity of Saskia's Flatbreads (see page
  196), to serve

01 Slice the aubergine into 5mm/¼ inch thick slices. Arrange the aubergine slices in your air fryer drawers, adding as many as you can fit in a single layer – you may have to cook them in batches. Spray the tops with the olive oil spray and season generously with salt and pepper. Set the temperature to 180°C/360°F and cook for 10 minutes, or until the aubergine is crispy and fork tender, then remove from the air fryer.

02 Put the lamb in the bottom of the air fryer drawer (removing the crisper plate first) and spread it out. Sprinkle the onion and oregano over the meat, and season with salt and pepper. Set the temperature to 180°C/360°F and cook for 5 minutes. Use a silicone spatula to break up the meat, then cook for a further 4 minutes.

03 When the air fryer beeps, stir the lamb again and add the passata, all the dried herbs and the garlic and tomato purées. Taste to check the seasoning, then tip it all into a bowl.

04 Dividing the mixture between two silicone containers that fit the dual drawers, start building up the moussaka layers. Start with a layer of sliced aubergine, a layer of the meat sauce (use it all), then another layer of aubergine.

05 Put the Bits and Bobs sauce in a mixing jug and add the grated Cheddar. Pour the sauce over the final layer of aubergine slices and sprinkle the top of the moussaka with the grated Parmesan. Place a crisper plate into each drawer and add a moussaka to each. Air fry for 8 minutes at 200°C/400°F, then serve with the flatbreads.

Basket moussaka Cook the aubergine/eggplant and meat sauce in the air fryer basket, then layer them up in a 20cm/8 inch round silicone container for the final cook.

Make ahead If making ahead, skip the 8 minute final cook time. Instead, layer up the moussaka in a silicone container and place in the fridge for up to 3 days. When ready to reheat, set the temperature to 160°C/320°F and cook for 30 minutes in the container, or until piping hot in the centre.

mezze wednesday: seriously good greek mezze

This is our go-to in the summer for a fun Greek tapas spread. We find that we often have many of the ingredients already, then we can prep whilst the air fryer cooks and get creative in putting together our mezze.

Plus, we have designed the mezze prep in a way that some items can be made ahead, so that it's not all to be done at once.

SERVES **4**
HERO **DUAL**
PREP **20 MINUTES**
COOK TIME **33 MINUTES**
CALORIES **819**

1 pot of shop-bought hummus
A few crispy chickpeas (see page 58)
1 recipe quantity Feta Cheese and Chive Dip (see page 143)
2 Saskia's Flatbreads (see page 196)
Extra virgin olive oil spray

FOR THE LAMB MEATBALLS
250g/9oz minced/ground lamb
¼ red onion, finely diced
1 tsp dried oregano, plus a sprinkling for the flatbreads
6 mint leaves, shredded
1 tsp garlic purée
2 tbsp panko breadcrumbs
1 small egg

FOR THE ROASTED VEGETABLES
1 red (bell) pepper/capsicum
½ aubergine/eggplant
¼ courgette/zucchini
1 tbsp extra virgin olive oil

1 tsp dried oregano
Salt and black pepper

FOR THE GREEK SALAD
85g/3oz/13 pitted mixed olives
¼ cucumber, sliced
¼ red onion, sliced
175g/6oz cherry tomatoes, halved
1 tbsp shredded fresh basil
1 tbsp extra virgin olive oil
1 tbsp white wine vinegar

01 Put all the meatball ingredients in a bowl, season with salt and pepper, and mix well with your hands, then divide it into 8 equal portions and roll them into meatballs (these can be prepped up to 3 days ahead).

02 The day you want to serve your mezze, transfer the meatballs straight from the fridge into the air fryer basket/drawer. Set the temperature to 180ºC/360ºF and cook for 14 minutes.

03 As your meatballs air fry, prepare your roasted vegetables. Chop the peppers into thick strips and put them in a mixing bowl. Cut the aubergine and courgette into 2cm/¾ inch dice and add to the bowl. Add the olive oil, oregano and a generous seasoning of salt and pepper, and mix with your hands.

04 When the air fryer beeps, remove the meatballs from the fryer. Tip the vegetables into the air fryer and, using the same temperature, cook for 15 minutes, or until the peppers look like they have been on the barbecue.

05 Meanwhile, put all the ingredients for the Greek salad in a bowl and mix well.

06 Start building your mezze spread. Put the hummus in a small serving bowl and top with a few crispy chickpeas, then put the feta dip in another small bowl. Put the meatballs and the roasted vegetables each in their own bowl.

07 For a finishing touch, slice the flatbreads into 3cm/1¼ inch wide strips. Spray with olive oil, sprinkle with dried oregano and air fry at 200ºC/400ºF for 4 minutes. Add to the selection and serve.

throwback thursday:
toad in the hole

If there is a comfort food I love the most, it is toad in the hole. Thick pork sausages are cooked in a Yorkshire pudding batter and are even easier and quicker thanks to the air fryer. We prefer our toad in the hole cooked in the dual air fryer because it makes a more traditional dish – and you can make one in each drawer. But it is also easily adapted to the air fryer basket (see our tip below).

....

SERVES **4**
HERO **DUAL**
PREP **5 MINUTES, PLUS RESTING**
COOK TIME **29 MINUTES**
CALORIES **743**

....

125g/4½oz/1 cup plain/all-purpose flour
2 large eggs
240ml/8fl oz/1 cup whole/full-fat milk
12 thick pork sausages
200ml/7fl oz/¾ cup beef gravy
225g/8oz frozen green beans
Salt and black pepper

01 Make the Yorkshire pudding batter 15 minutes before you place the sausages in the air fryer, because the batter needs to sit for at least 20 minutes. Put the flour in a mixing bowl and season with salt and pepper. Make a well in the centre of the flour and crack the eggs into the well, then mix with a fork until well combined. Gradually add the milk, mixing until bubbles form in your batter and it's a similar consistency to pancake batter. Put it to one side and let it rest for 15 minutes.

02 Remove the crisper plate from the two air fryer drawers and divide the sausages between the drawers, placing six in each. Cook at 200ºC/400ºF for 8 minutes. When the air fryer beeps, turn the sausages over with tongs, then quickly pour the Yorkshire pudding batter over the sausages. Air fry at the same temperature for a further 8 minutes.

03 When the air fryer beeps, use a plate to flip both the toad in the holes over – this will help the bottoms to crisp up. Air fry at 200ºC/400ºF for another 5 minutes, or until golden to your liking.

04 When the air fryer beeps, remove the toad in the holes from each drawer and add the crisper plates back in. Pour your gravy into a ramekin and put it in one of the drawers, then add the frozen green beans to the other drawer. Match the air fryer drawers and cook at 180ºC/360ºF for 8 minutes or until the green beans and gravy are piping hot.

05 Slice each toad in the hole in half so that there are three sausages in each portion, then serve with green beans and gravy.

Toad in the basket Divide the ingredients between two 20cm/8 inch silicone containers, each 5cm/2 inches deep. Cook them one at a time following the times and temperatures above.

Fatty sausages It's important that you use full fat sausages and avoid low-fat varieties. This is because the fat from the sausages is what helps the toad in the hole to cook.

friday fish supper: dom's fish burgers

These fish burgers are delicious – they're like having crispy breaded fish in a burger bun. It adds something different to your Friday night fakeaway. Serve them with our skin-on French fries (see page 154) for a proper burger and chips weekend spread.

....

SERVES **2**
HERO **BASKET/DUAL**
PREP **10 MINUTES**
COOK TIME **8 MINUTES**
CALORIES **786**

....

35g/1¼oz/¼ cup plain/all-purpose flour
1 tbsp dried basil
1 large egg, beaten
2 tsp lemon juice
55g/2oz/½ cup golden breadcrumbs
1 tbsp dried parsley
2 × 110g/3¾oz white fish fillets
1 tbsp dried dill
2 brioche bread buns or rolls, sliced in half
A few lettuce leaves
2 slices processed burger cheese
½ tomato, sliced
Salt and black pepper

FOR THE DILL SAUCE
2 tsp finely chopped fresh dill
2 tbsp mayonnaise
½ tsp garlic purée
4 tbsp Greek yoghurt
2 tsp lemon juice

01 First set up a production line. Put the flour in a shallow bowl and stir in the basil. Put the beaten egg in another bowl and stir in the lemon juice. Put the breadcrumbs in a third bowl and add the parsley. Give each bowl a generous seasoning of salt and pepper, and also season the fish fillets with salt and pepper too. Add a sprinkling of dill to both sides of the fish fillets, then you're ready for breading.

02 First, turn the fish over in the flour to fully coat, then drench them in the egg. Finish with a double coating in the breadcrumbs.

03 Place the breaded fish fillets into the air fryer basket/drawer, set the temperature to 180ºC/360ºF and cook for 8 minutes, or until cooked through.

04 In the meantime, mix together the dill sauce ingredients in a small bowl.

05 When the air fryer beeps, you can assemble the burgers. Spread a thick layer of dill sauce over the bottom halves of the buns, then add some shredded lettuce and a fish fillet. Top the fish with a slice of cheese, then add a couple of tomato slices before putting the bun lids on top and serving straight away.

Frugal fakeaway Frozen fish fillets are usually cheaper than fresh ones. We use frozen pollock that we thaw before following the recipe above. Other great choices include filleted basa/catfish and tilapia. If using frozen, pat dry with kitchen paper/paper towel first.

saturday fakeaway: chicken tikka masala with bombay potatoes & naan

This chicken curry tastes amazing, it is easy to prepare, includes a hidden veggie curry sauce and is freezer friendly too. Best of all, it takes just 18 minutes to air fry.

SERVES **2**
HERO **BASKET/DUAL**
PREP **10 MINUTES**
COOK TIME **18 MINUTES**
CALORIES **1175**

675g/1½ lb boneless skinless chicken thighs
Extra virgin olive oil spray
2 tsp ground cumin
½ tsp ground turmeric
2 tsp ground coriander
2 tsp smoked paprika
½ tsp ground ginger
½ tsp garlic powder
Salt and black pepper

FOR TIKKA MASALA SAUCE
1 recipe quantity Butternut Squash Curry Sauce
 (see page 175)
1 tbsp tikka masala curry paste
2 tbsp passata
1 tsp tomato purée/paste
1 tsp garlic purée
1 tsp ginger purée

TO SERVE
Make-ahead Bombay Potatoes (see page 159)
Garlic and Coriander Naan (see page 130)
Thick yoghurt (optional)

01 Slice the chicken thighs into quarters, creating large chunks of chicken. Spray them with olive oil to create a sticky texture, then put them into a mixing bowl. Add all the dried spices, season generously with salt and pepper, and mix well with your hands.

02 Place the seasoned chicken into the air fryer basket/drawer. Set the temperature to 180°C/360°F and cook for 12 minutes, or until the chicken reaches an internal temperature of 70°C/160°F or above.

03 Put the butternut squash curry sauce in a mixing bowl and add the tikka masala paste, passata and the tomato, garlic and ginger purées. Stir everything together well.

04 Transfer the cooked chicken to the curry sauce bowl and toss to coat. Transfer to the dual drawer (without the crisper plate) or if you are using a basket air fryer, tip it into a silicone container. Cook at the same temperature for a further 6 minutes, or until the sauce is heated through and has slightly reduced.

05 Serve the chicken tikka masala with the Bombay potatoes, and warm naan bread – and yoghurt, if you like.

Don't want to make naan bread? You can reheat shop bought naan bread in the air fryer. Cook from frozen at 200°C/400°F for 4 minutes, or from room temperature at 180°C/360°F for 3 minutes for a quick warm through.

sunday roast:
rosemary leg of lamb with carrots, potatoes & peas

For the ultimate Sunday roast dinner, this lamb roast ticks all the boxes. Made with a small bone-in leg of lamb, goose fat roast potatoes, thyme flavoured carrots and minted peas, it looks amazing, yet is as simple as you can get.

SERVES **4**
HERO **BASKET/DUAL**
PREP **15 MINUTES**
COOK TIME **65 MINUTES**
CALORIES **604**

1.3kg/3lb bone-in leg of lamb
Extra virgin olive oil spray
2 tsp dried rosemary
1 garlic bulb
6 medium potatoes
2 tsp goose fat/duck fat
1 tbsp dried thyme
4 medium carrots
1 tsp extra virgin olive oil
1 tbsp mixed herbs/Italian seasoning
200g/7oz/1½ cups frozen garden peas
5 mint leaves, thinly shredded
1 tsp mint sauce
1 tsp salted butter
Salt and black pepper

01 Spray the lamb leg with olive oil, then rub the dried rosemary and a generous seasoning of salt and pepper all over the lamb. Carefully place the lamb leg into the air fryer basket/drawer. Slice the top off your garlic bulb and then spray a little olive oil on top and sprinkle with salt and pepper. Wrap the garlic in foil and place in the air fryer basket/drawer with the lamb leg. Cook at 180°C/360°F for 25 minutes.

02 While the lamb is cooking, prepare the sides. For the potatoes, peel, then slice each in half. Put the potatoes in a bowl and add the goose fat and the dried thyme, season with salt and pepper and mix with your hands. Put it to one side.

03 Next, peel and slice the carrots into quarters – we find slicing them diagonally works well for an even cook. Put the carrots into a mixing bowl with the olive oil, and dried mixed herbs. Season with salt and pepper and mix well with your hands.

04 When the air fryer beeps, turn the the lamb over. Remove the garlic bulb from the foil and squeeze the soft cloves out of the skin. Add half the garlic to each bowl of veggies and mix both with your hands. Scatter the potatoes and carrots into the gaps around the lamb (or into the second drawer if using a dual). Keep the temperature at 180°C/360°F and air fry for a further 25 minutes.

05 When the air fryer beeps, check the internal temperature (see tip below), then remove the lamb, place it on a plate and cover with foil to allow it to rest. In the meantime, spread the carrots and potatoes out in the air fryer basket/drawer and air fry for a further 10 minutes.

06 While waiting on the carrots and potatoes, put the frozen peas, fresh mint, mint sauce and butter into a silicone container. Season with salt and pepper, and mix with a spoon.

07 When the air fryer beeps, swap the potatoes and carrots for the peas and air fry at the same temperature for 5 minutes, or until the peas are heated through and the butter has melted. Your lamb leg dinner is now ready for serving.

Use a thermometer This is important to avoid overcooking your lamb. For "medium" you need an internal temperature to 53°C/127°F. This is medium-rare, but as the lamb rests, it will continue to cook in the residual heat for a short time and will increase by 9°C/48°F.

BAKING

let's air fry flatbread

Known as two-ingredient yoghurt dough in the air fryer communities, this flatbread-style dough is perfect for the many different air fryer recipes where you need a simple dough to use in multiple ways. Master this flatbread dough, then with the recipes in this book, make bagels, pasties and – our personal favourite – naan bread. This dough also freezes well.

saskia's flatbreads (& two-ingredient dough)

SERVES **4 FLATBREADS**
HERO **BASKET/DUAL**
PREP **10 MINUTES**
COOK TIME **6 MINUTES**
CALORIES **252**

225g/8oz/1¾ cups plain flour/ all-purpose flour, plus extra for dusting
250g/9oz/1 cup fat-free Greek yoghurt

I first tried recipes for this two-ingredient dough six years ago when it became an air fryer trend. I hated it; either the dough was too dry from too much flour, or too wet from too much yoghurt. Then Saskia, my baking teacher, taught me the perfect ratio of 90 per cent flour to yoghurt, and since then it's been my go-to dough. Thank you Saskia. Once you've mastered the basic dough, you can also add any flavourings you wish – see our tip box opposite.

01 Sift the flour into a mixing bowl and add the yoghurt. Use the back of a wooden spoon to press the yoghurt into the flour to help combine the two ingredients, then stir together with the wooden spoon until coming together into a dough.

02 Flour a clean worktop, your hands, and your rolling pin, then tip the dough onto your worktop. With your floured hands, knead the dough for a couple of minutes, gathering in any little bits of mixture that haven't combined as you knead, until you have a smooth dough.

03 Divide the dough into four equal portions and roll one out at a time to an oval shape of a flatbread (or if you have a small air fryer, just roll it to the size and shape that will fit in your fryer).

04 Carefully place a flatbread into the air fryer basket, or you can place one in each drawer if you have a dual. Set the temperature to 180°C/360°F and cook for 4 minutes, then flip over and cook for another 2 minutes, or until the flatbread is golden to your liking. Repeat to cook the rest of the flatbreads. Note that they will puff up slightly as they cook and will naturally flatten after a couple of minutes resting time.

Just the dough If a recipe in the book calls for Saskia's Two-Ingredient Dough, prepare it following steps 1 and 2, then continue as directed in the recipe.

Top tips

Naturally sticky dough Because it's a combo of yoghurt and flour, the dough is naturally sticky. This is okay, but you just need to be patient when handling the dough – make sure your hands are floured to stop them sticking and avoid the temptation to over-flour your dough.

Flavour your flatbread After starting with just two ingredients, the dough can be any flavour you want it to be. We recommend a teaspoon of garlic purée along with a teaspoon of any favourite dried herb or spice. Or why not use half a teaspoon each of two favourites, such as dried basil and dried oregano?

Freezing the dough This flatbread dough freezes perfectly and is ideal for when you expect to have leftover dough or you want it ready-made for next time. Simply roll out the flatbreads as above, then freeze on an oven tray that is laid flat in the freezer. (Freezing flat before bagging like this stops the dough sticking together.) Once frozen, load the raw flatbreads into freezer bags.

Saskia's pinch pot At baking class, Saskia has what she calls a flour pinch pot. This is brilliant for baking with sticky dough as you can flour your sticky hands without having to put them into your clean flour bag. Simply fill a small bowl with flour and have it on the worktop next to you for quick access.

Self-raising flour swap If you want your dough to rise, such as for the bagels (see page 198), swap the plain/all-purpose flour for self-raising/self-rising flour.

the easiest bagels recipe ever

Love warm bagels? Then transform a batch of this yoghurt dough into bagels, mixing and matching with your favourite toppings and fillings.

....

MAKES **4**
HERO **BASKET/DUAL**
PREP **5 MINUTES**
COOK TIME **16 MINUTES**
CALORIES **266**

....

Plain/all-purpose flour, for
  dusting
1 recipe quantity Saskia's Two-
  Ingredient Dough (see page
  196), made using self-raising/
  self-rising flour,
  at room temperature
1 small egg, beaten
2 tsp bagel seasoning

01 Dust a clean worktop with flour, and lightly dust your rolling pin. Flour your hands, too, to stop the dough sticking to them.

02 Knead the dough, then divide it into four equal portions and shape them into balls. Stick your finger in the flour to dust it, then insert it into the centre of one of the balls and wiggle it around firmly until you have a large hole, about 3cm/1¼ inch wide. You could also use a small cookie cutter for this, if you prefer. Repeat until you have shaped all four bagels.

03 Brush the tops of the bagels with the beaten egg, then sprinkle with the bagel seasoning.

04 Place the bagels into the air fryer – you should be able to fit all four in one air fryer basket or, if you have a dual fryer, place two in each drawer. Set the temperature to 180ºC/360ºF and cook for 8 minutes.

05 When the air fryer beeps, reduce the temperature to 160ºC/320ºF and cook for a further 8 minutes. They should be cooked, but If the bottoms aren't firm, flip them over and cook for another 2 minutes to crisp up the bases. Serve warm with your favourite fillings.

Bagel bites If you are using a small cookie cutter to create your bagel shapes, you can make little bagel bites from your leftover bagel holes. Brush them with egg wash, then put them in the air fryer, spreading them out for an even cook, and air fry at 180ºC/360ºF for 5 minutes.

cheese, onion & potato pasties

As a kid, I loved visiting the local bakery. The sausage rolls, flapjacks and warm cheese and potato pasties always caught my eye. Clearly, they made a lasting impression as all three are in this chapter! We are using the yoghurt dough as an easy method for recreating those pasties in the air fryer.

....

MAKES **4**
HERO **BASKET/DUAL**
PREP **10 MINUTES**
COOK TIME **28 MINUTES**
CALORIES **562**

....

1 large baking potato
1 spring onion/scallion
2 tsp extra virgin olive oil
¼ tsp mustard powder
2 tsp mixed herbs/Italian seasoning
1 recipe quantity Saskia's Two-Ingredient Dough (see page 196), at room temperature
Plain/all-purpose flour, for dusting
4 tbsp sour cream
115g/4oz/1¼ cups grated mature/sharp Cheddar cheese
1 egg, beaten
Salt and black pepper

01 Peel the potato and dice it into 1cm/½ inch cubes. Clean and slice the spring onion. Put both into a bowl and add the olive oil and half each of the mustard and the mixed herbs. Season with salt and pepper, and mix with your hands until the potato and onion are well coated in the oil and seasonings. Transfer just the potato cubes to the air fryer basket/drawer, set the temperature to 180ºC/360ºF and cook for 10 minutes. Then tip the onion into the air fryer with the potatoes and cook for a further 8 minutes.

02 In the meantime get your pasty dough ready. Dust a clean worktop with flour, and lightly dust your rolling pin. Flour your hands, too, to stop the dough sticking to them. Roll the dough to a sheet 5mm/¼ inch thick. Use the back of a pasty maker to make four dough circles. You will need to gather up the scraps and re-roll the dough to make the fourth circle.

03 When the air fryer beeps, tip the potato and onion into a mixing bowl. Add the sour cream, cheese, and the remaining seasonings and mix well with a spoon.

04 Flour the dough discs on both sides, then also flour the pasty maker to prevent sticking. Add a dough round to the pasty maker, then add one-quarter of the filling. Use the pasty maker to fold one side of the dough over to make a semi-circular pasty, then gently remove it from the pasty maker. Repeat the process to fill the other three pasties.

05 Using a pastry brush, egg wash the tops of your pasties. Place two pasties into the air fryer basket, or one in each drawer if using the dual air fryer. Set the temperature to 180ºC/360ºF and cook for 10 minutes, or until piping hot throughout. Repeat to cook the remaining two pasties and serve warm.

Use a cookie cutter If you don't have a pasty maker, you can still make these. Simply roll out the dough and cut out the rounds with a 15cm/6 inch cookie cutter. Add a spoonful of filling to the dough round and fold over to create a semi-circular pasty, then crimp the edges with a fork to seal.

Cooking from frozen If you prefer air frying raw pasties from frozen (shop-bought or your own), add them to the air fryer basket/drawer still frozen and air fry at 160ºC/320ºF for 6 minutes, followed by 200ºC/400ºF for 4 minutes, or until piping hot.

homemade sausage rolls

Sausage rolls in the air fryer are a must. You can make full sized sausage rolls like the bakery, or make smaller mini sausage rolls for parties. We love to have them in the summer for picnics, for afternoon tea or as a midmorning snack on Christmas Day.

....

MAKES **4**
HERO **BASKET/DUAL**
PREP **8 MINUTES**
COOK TIME **13 MINUTES**
CALORIES **482**

....

Plain/all-purpose flour, for dusting
½ x 500g/1lb 2oz block of puff pastry (freeze the rest for another day)
1 tbsp tomato purée/paste
1 tsp dried thyme
325g/11½oz seasoned sausage meat (or remove the skin from pork sausages)
1 egg, beaten for egg wash
Ketchup, to serve (optional)

01 Dust a clean worktop and a rolling pin with flour. Roll out the puff pastry into a large rectangle measuring 30 × 20cm/12 × 8 inches. Cut the rectangle in half lengthways to create two long pastry strips.

02 Spread a layer of tomato purée over the centre pastry strips (we find this is easiest to do with a pastry brush), leaving a 1cm/½ inch gap around the edges of each for the egg wash. Sprinkle the dried thyme over the purée.

03 Divide the sausagemeat into two portions and roll each one out into a sausage shape 30cm/12 inches long. Place a sausage down the length of each pastry strip.

04 Brush egg wash around the bare edge of the dough, then fold the dough over to make a long sausage roll. Crimp down the edge of the log with a fork to seal it, then repeat to fold the other roll. Use a sharp knife to cut each sausage roll in half to make four large sausage rolls, then make a number of small slashes across the top of the rolls so that the steam can escape during cooking.

05 Carefully place the sausage rolls into the air fryer basket/drawer, spreading them out. I can normally fit four sausage rolls in a basket, or two in each dual drawer. Brush the tops of the rolls with egg wash.

06 Set the temperature to 180ºC/360ºF and cook for 10 minutes. Brush them with a little more egg wash, then cook for another 3 minutes, or until cooked through and golden. Serve warm or cold – they are delicious with ketchup.

Make party rolls If you want smaller sausage rolls for a party, simply cut them smaller. Once you have cut them into four, cut each one into quarters, so that you have 16 party-sized rolls. If cooking party sausage rolls, a total cook time of 8 minutes will be perfect.

golden syrup flapjacks

Whether you live in the UK and call them flapjacks or live in the USA and call them granola bars, they are one of the easiest air fryer recipes. If you don't like golden syrup, you can swap it for the same quantity of maple syrup or honey.

SERVES **8**
HERO **BASKET**
PREP **8 MINUTES**
COOK TIME **24 MINUTES**
CALORIES **303**

115g/4oz/½ cup unsalted
   butter
2 tbsp golden syrup/light corn
   syrup
100g/3½oz/½ cup light brown
   sugar
250g/9oz/2½ cups porridge/
   rolled oats

01 Put the butter into a 20cm/8 inch silicone pan, cutting it into bite-sized cubes as you add it. Add the golden syrup, then transfer the pan to the air fryer basket. Set the temperature to 120°C/250°F and cook for 4 minutes, or until the butter has melted.

02 Add the brown sugar and the oats to the pan and stir everything together well. Spread the mixture out evenly over the base of the pan, then flatten down firmly with the back of a spoon.

03 Increase the temperature to 150°C/300°F and cook for 20 minutes. Let it sit in the warm air fryer for another 5 minutes, then let them cool completely at room temperature before transferring to the fridge to chill for an hour. Slice the flapjack into eight wedges before serving.

Dual flapjacks Follow the recipe above, but swap the round silicone pans for two smaller rectangular containers that fit the dual drawers and divide the mixture between the two. Or reduce your washing up and use foil trays/pans!

veronica's coconut oatmeal cookies

My aunt made these for us, and after just one bite, I asked for the recipe. She compiled a cookbook of her best recipes for me, including these delicious oatmeal cookies. The recipe was passed down to her from a local farmer's wife and it's now my pleasure to pass the recipe on to you, adapted for the air fryer, of course!

....

MAKES **16**
HERO **BASKET/DUAL**
PREP **10 MINUTES**
COOK TIME **12 MINUTES**
CALORIES **272**

....

175g/6oz/¾ cup unsalted butter
2 tbsp golden syrup/light corn syrup
110g/3¾oz/1¼ cups desiccated/dried shredded coconut
125g/4½oz/1¼ cups porridge/rolled oats
200g/7oz/1 cup granulated sugar
170g/6oz/1¼ cups self-raising/self-rising flour
2 tsp ground ginger

01 Put the butter into a silicone pan, cutting it into bite-sized cubes as you add it. Add the golden syrup, then transfer the pan to the air fryer basket/drawer. Set the temperature to 120°C/250°F and cook for 4 minutes, or until the butter has melted.

02 Transfer the butter and golden syrup to a mixing bowl and add the coconut, oats and sugar. Mix well with a wooden spoon. Gradually add the flour and the ground ginger, then use your hands to continue mixing until everything is combined and you have a cookie dough.

03 Divide the oatmeal dough into 16 portions and roll each into a ball. We found the easiest way is to use an ice cream scoop. Then you can scoop each oatmeal cookie mix into the perfect ball.

04 Because this recipe makes 16, we air fry them in batches. Place four cookies into the air fryer basket, spreading them out, or place two in each drawer if you are using a dual air fryer. Set the temperature to 180°C/360°F and cook for 8 minutes, or until golden. Allow to rest for 5 minutes to firm up before eating.

Make ahead If you like, you can freeze the raw dough for later, so you can have cookies in an instant! Prepare the dough as above, then spread out the cookies on a baking tray and place them flat in the freezer for an hour. Once they have firmed up, transfer to a freezer bag. This will stop them sticking together as they freeze. To cook, place as many frozen cookies as you would like to cook into the air fryer and air fry at 160°C/320°F for 10 minutes.

road trip raspberry & white chocolate muffins

If we are off travelling, I can guarantee these muffins will be made the day before and stored in Tupperware for those "I'm starving" moments. Whether it's on a road trip or on a plane, these travel so well.

....

MAKES **20**
HERO **BASKET/DUAL**
PREP **10 MINUTES**
COOK TIME **20 MINUTES**
CALORIES **171**

....

75g/2½oz/⅓ cup unsalted butter
1 large egg
150g/5½oz/¾ cup granulated sugar
250g/9oz/1 cup Greek yoghurt
1 tbsp vanilla extract
4 tbsp whole milk/full-fat milk
250g/9oz/2 cups self-raising/ self-rising flour
180g/6¼oz raspberries, chopped
170g/6oz/1 cup white chocolate chunks

01 Put the butter into a silicone pan, cutting it into bite-sized cubes as you add it. Transfer the pan to the air fryer basket, set the temperature to 120°C/250°F and cook for 4 minutes, or until the butter has melted.

02 Carefully transfer the melted butter to a mixing bowl and add the egg and sugar. Beat with a hand whisk until nice and creamy.

03 Add the yoghurt, vanilla and milk, and continue to mix with the whisk until you have a smooth and creamy batter. Gradually add the flour, continuing to mix as you add it. Finish by adding the chopped fruit and chocolate chunks and stirring to combine.

04 Use an ice cream scoop to add a scoop of the muffin batter into silicone muffin cups. Fill as many cups as will fit in your air fryer (I can normally fit 8 in my air fryer basket).

05 Set the temperature to 170°C/340°F and cook for 10 minutes, then cover with foil and air fry at 180°C/360°F for a further 5 minutes, or until a thermometer probe inserted into the centre of the muffins comes out clean.

06 While they are cooking, fill more cups (or you may need to wait until a batch is cooked and wash and reuse the cups, depending on how many you have). Continue to cook them in batches until all the muffins are cooked. Once cool, store in an airtight container and they will keep for up to 5 days – unless the kids raid the Tupperware without you noticing!

Dual muffins If you are making these in the dual, melt the butter in a silicone pan in a dual drawer and continue with the recipe above. Load the muffins into the drawers (we can usually fit 6 in each drawer) and set the temperature to 160°C/320°F. Cook for 10 minutes, then cover them with foil and cook at 180°C/360°F for a further 10 minutes. This is because we find they brown slightly more on top in the dual.

Mix and match This recipe works well with 180g/6¼oz of any berries – although if you are using large ones, like strawberries, chop them up first. Dom's favourite is blueberries (in photo, left), though Sofia and I love a mix of strawberries and raspberries. Or if you fancy a bit of both, separate the mixture into two bowls before adding the fruit and you can do half a batch with a mixture of strawberries and raspberries and half a batch with blueberries.

let's air fry a cheesecake

If you love cheesecake, you will love a baked cheesecake in the air fryer. The mixture is whipped up fast thanks to an electric hand mixer.
You can also use the air fryer for melting the butter for the cheesecake crust, as well as for melting the chocolate for decorating the cheesecake.

the ultimate baked cheesecake

SERVES **8**
HERO **BASKET**
PREP **10 MINUTES**
COOK TIME **37 MINUTES**
CALORIES **718**

....

FOR THE COOKIE BASE
60g/2oz/¼ cup unsalted butter
200g/7oz chocolate sandwich
  cookies (we use Oreos)

FOR THE CHEESECAKE LAYER
700g/1lb 9oz full-fat cream
  cheese (we use Original
  Philadelphia)
250g/9oz/1¼ cups granulated
  sugar
3 tbsp sour cream
2 tsp vanilla extract
2 large eggs
100g/3½oz chocolate sandwich
  cookies (we use Oreos)

TO DECORATE
75g/2½oz/½ cup white
  chocolate chunks
2–3 snack bags of mini chocolate
  sandwich cookies (we use
  about 50g/1¾oz of Mini Oreos)

We flavour our easy air fryer cheesecake with Oreos. They make the delicious chocolate biscuit base and are crumbled into the batter, so you get a brilliant effect as you slice through. If you can find bags of the mini ones, they make the cutest decoration for the top, too.

....

01 Place a silicone pan into the air fryer basket and add the butter, cutting it into bite-sized cubes as you add it. Set the temperature to 120°C/250°F and air fry for 4 minutes, or until the butter is melted.

02 Put the cookies for the base in a mixing bowl and crush them with a rolling pin, until they are crumbs and you have no big bits left. When the air fryer beeps, transfer the melted butter to the mixing bowl with the crushed Oreos. Mix well with a fork. Tip the buttery crumbs into the bottom of a 18cm/7 inch springform pan and spread level. Press down to compact it – we always find a potato masher is useful for this – making sure it is level.

03 Put the cream cheese and sugar in a large mixing bowl and beat with an electric hand mixer on medium speed until well combined and very creamy. Add the sour cream and vanilla, and continue to mix, then add the eggs, one at a time, mixing in between each egg.

04 Finally, add the cookies, breaking them in half as you add them. Use the mixer to naturally break them down a bit more into various sizes, but don't let them get too small, as it's nice to see chunks of cookie as you slice the finished cheesecake.

05 Tip the batter over the crumb base in your pan and use the back of a spatula to level the top. Carefully place the pan into the air fryer basket. Set the temperature to 160°C/320°F and cook for 30 minutes.

CONTINUED OVERLEAF
....

06 When the air fryer beeps, use a thermometer probe to check that the temperature in the middle of the cheesecake is 70ºC/160ºF or above, and that the thermometer probe comes out clean. (If it isn't the correct temperature, give it another 5 minutes and then test again until it is at the required internal temperature.) Close the air fryer basket, and let it sit for another 30 minutes in the cooling air fryer, as the residual heat will continue the setting process. Once completely cool, transfer the cheesecake to the fridge and allow it to chill for 12 hours before decorating and slicing.

07 To decorate, put two-thirds of the white chocolate chunks into a silicone pan and air fry at 120ºC/250ºF for 3 minutes, or until melted. Transfer the chocolate to a piping bag and snip off the end to make a tiny hole. Drizzle the chocolate over the top of the cheesecake.

08 Use the mini cookies to decorate around the edge of the cheesecake – the melted chocolate will help secure them in place. Add some whole, but break others up to vary the look. Finish by scattering over the remaining chocolate chunks.

....

Dual cheesecake If using a dual air fryer, you wont be able to fit a 18cm/7 inch springform pan in. Instead, halve the quantities of the crust and cheesecake batter ingredients, and divide them between four 10cm/4 inch springform pans. Place two pans in each drawer and cook as in the main recipe, but reducing the cook time to 20 minutes. You can also save time by using the "match" feature.

Top tips

Easy crushing To crush the cookies easily, use the end of a rolling pin, standing it up and pressing down into the cookies in the bowl to make crumbs.

Use the right pan It's important that you use the right size pan, as this will determine the thickness of your cheesecake topping and make sure the cooking time is correct. If you use a smaller pan, the cheesecake layer will be deeper and it won't be set within the cooking time.

Perfect slicing To get a smooth edge to your slices, heat your knife in a jug of hot water and wipe off the water and slice whilst still hot. It will melt the cheesecake layer slightly as it goes through, creating the perfect slice.

Alarm It's easy to forget about your cheesecake when you're leaving it to cool in the air fryer before moving it to the fridge. We set an alarm on our Alexa.

Use ramekins instead This cheesecake recipe can also be made in ramekin dishes – perfect for if you want a quicker cooking method. Make the crumb crust and cheesecake batter as in the main recipe, but divide both mixtures between eight ramekins. Reduce the cook time to 15 minutes at 160ºC/320ºF, followed by a 15 minute cool down in the air fryer. An average-sized air fryer will hold four ramekins, meaning you would only need to do two batches.

Smaller air fryers If you have a small air fryer, using ramekins makes it possible for you to cook cheesecake too. You can usually fit in two ramekins at once, so this is a good solution if your air fryer is too small for a springform pan.

vanilla sprinkle cake

I loved puddings when I was little at school. Even now in my forties I want to recreate them in the air fryer. Top of the list, and also our kids' favourite, is a vanilla sprinkle cake. Made with a vanilla sponge, pink icing and, of course, plenty of sprinkles.

....

SERVES **8**
HERO **BASKET**
PREP **10 MINUTES**
COOK TIME **60 MINUTES**
CALORIES **510**

....

170g/6oz/¾ cup unsalted
  butter
200g/7oz/1 cup granulated
  sugar
4 large eggs
1 tbsp vanilla extract
6 tbsp whole milk/full-fat milk
1½ tbsp extra virgin olive oil
180g/6¼oz/1⅓ cups self-
  raising/self-rising flour
100g/3½oz/¾ cup icing/
  confectioner's sugar
⅓ tsp hot pink food colouring
  (or any colour you like)
2½ tbsp rainbow sprinkles

01 Put the butter and sugar in a mixing bowl and, using an electric hand mixer, beat until it becomes almost white and has a fluffy texture. Crack the eggs into the bowl, add the vanilla, milk and olive oil, and continue to whisk until smooth and creamy.

02 Sift in the flour, a bit at a time, folding it in and not over-mixing because you want a light and fluffy cake. Then pour the mixture into a 20cm/8 inch round silicone pan and place it carefully into the air fryer basket.

03 Set the temperature to 160ºC/320ºF and cook for 30 minutes. When the air fryer beeps, cover the cake in foil to prevent it over-browning on top and cook at 150ºC/300ºF for another 30 minutes, or until a thermometer probe inserted into the centre of the cake comes out clean.

04 Remove the silicone pan – it will easily peel away from the cake – and place the cake on a cooling rack to cool completely before icing.

05 Sift the icing sugar into a mixing bowl and add about 2 tablespoons water – a little at a time – mixing until you have the consistency of a thick paste. Add the food colouring a little at a time, mixing until you have the shade of pink you want. Just remember to add it slowly, because you can always add more but you can't take it away.

06 Pour the pink icing over the cooled cake, then cover it with sprinkles and leave to set. Once set, slice and serve.

Dual sprinkle cake If you have a dual air fryer, you won't be able to fit the specified cake pan in the drawer. Instead, divide the batter between four 10cm/4 inch cake tins and cook two pans in each drawer at 160ºC/320ºF for 30 minutes.

three-ingredient shortbread

I love shortbread. As a kid, every Christmas my parents' Scottish bookkeeper would gift us some shortbread. I thought it was the nicest treat ever. As a grown-up I learnt it was ridiculously easy to make and could be used in many recipes.

Let me first show you our master recipe for Scottish shortbread, and then how to transform it into chocolate orange shortbread, and strawberries and cream shortbread stacks.

SERVES **8**
HERO **BASKET**
PREP **5 MINUTES**
COOK TIME **35 MINUTES**
CALORIES **314**

240g/8¼oz/1¾ cups plain/all-purpose flour
75g/3oz/6 tbsp granulated sugar, plus extra for sprinkling
175g/6oz/¾ cup unsalted butter

01 Put the flour, sugar and butter in a mixing bowl. Use your fingertips to rub the fat into the flour, continuing until big lumps form, then bring the mixture together into a dough. The high fat content means that it forms into a dough easily; try not to over-handle the dough, because the butter will get too melty.

02 Place the dough into a 20cm/8 inch round silicone cake pan and press it down, so that it creates an even disc in the base of the silicone pan. Use a fork to crimp around the edge, like traditional shortbread and score the top to divide it into 8 wedges. Doing so now will create the lines to slice again when cooked and makes it much easier.

03 Place the silicone pan in the air fryer basket, set the temperature to 150ºC/300ºF and cook for 20 minutes. Increase the temperature to 180ºC/360ºF and cook for a further 15 minutes until light golden.

04 Remove the silicone pan from the air fryer and sprinkle the shortbread with extra sugar. Allow to rest before peeling away from the silicone. Use the original cuts as your guide to slice into eight "petticoat tails" before serving.

Smaller shortbreads As this classic shortbread won't fit the air fryer dual drawers or into a small air fryer, we recommend using a cookie cutter and making individual shortbread rounds instead. You can follow our recipe on page 217 and either enjoy as plain cookies or transform it into a strawberry and cream dessert.

Tip We find that the easiest way to press our shortbread dough down firmly into the tin is to use a potato masher.

Hot chocolate orange shortbread This is our favourite way to make shortbread and a chocolaty upgrade of traditional Scottish shortbread. Make as above, but as you add the main ingredients to the bowl, add an extra **28g/1oz/3 tablespoons plain/all-purpose flour, 60g/2oz/½ cup hot chocolate powder** and the **finely grated zest of a medium orange**, plus **2 tablespoons of the orange juice**.

strawberry shortbread stacks

Shortbread cookies are made from the shortbread dough on page 214, then loaded with fresh strawberries, and whipped cream.

SERVES **6**
HERO **BASKET/DUAL**
PREP **8 MINUTES**
COOK TIME **30 MINUTES**
CALORIES **649**

1 recipe quantity of shortbread dough (see ingredients and step 1 on page 214, but don't shape the dough)
Plain/all-purpose flour, for dusting
225g/8oz fresh strawberries
fresh mint sprigs, to decorate

CHANTILLY CREAM
240ml/8fl oz/1 cup double/ heavy cream
1 tsp vanilla extract
2 tbsp icing/confectioners' sugar, plus extra for dusting

01 Make the shortbread dough as in the recipe on page 214. Use your hands to knead everything together, then lightly flour a worktop and press the dough out to form a sheet 5mm/¼ inch thick. Using a 7cm/2¾ inch cookie cutter, stamp out 12 rounds – you will need to gather up the offcuts and reroll to make all 12 rounds. Place 4 shortbread cookies into the air fryer basket, or if using the drawers of a dual add 3 to each drawer.

02 Set the temperature to 180ºC/360ºF and cook for 10 minutes until light golden. Allow to cool on a cooling rack while you cook the remaining shortbreads. Allow all the shortbreads to cool completely before moving on to the next step.

03 Put the cream into a mixing bowl and add the vanilla extract and icing sugar. Using an electric hand mixer, whip the cream to soft peaks.

04 Slice the strawberries. Add a good spoonful of the chantilly cream to the top of six of the shortbread rounds, then top with some of the sliced strawberries. Add another shortbread on top of each stack and top it with more cream and strawberries. Add a sprig of mint to each to decorate, and dust the tops with icing sugar.

The sweetest strawberries There is nothing like strawberries in season, but at other times, they sometimes need a little help. Put your strawberries in a bowl and sprinkle over **2 tablespoons granulated sugar**. Mix well and leave to macerate for a couple of hours to soften and sweeten the fruit.

Strawberry cream You can also make the cream in these stacks strawberry flavoured, if you wish. Finely chop a couple of your sweetened strawberries and add them to the cream with the vanilla and sugar. Whisk for a few seconds until the strawberries have combined and the cream is a lovely shade of pink. If you'd like it pinker, add a few more strawberries, but be careful not to overwhip the cream or it may go grainy.

afternoon tea with classic scones

For the last recipe, we're combining some of our favourite recipes from this book to bring you an amazing air fryer afternoon tea.

lemonade scones

You can't have afternoon tea without scones! Let's first share our five-ingredient scones recipe, before running through some ideas of what to pair these scones with for your afternoon tea.

MAKES **6**
HERO **BASKET/DUAL**
PREP **8 MINUTES**
COOK TIME **14 MINUTES**
CALORIES **330**

340g/11¾oz/2½ cups self-raising/self-rising flour, plus extra for dusting
85g/3oz/7 tbsp granulated sugar
120ml/4fl oz/½ cup lemonade
120g/4¼oz/½ cup Greek yoghurt
85g/3oz raisins or sultanas
1 egg, beaten for egg wash

serving suggestions

For a traditional afternoon tea for two, we recommend you fill the top layer of a cake stand with scones; sweet treats occupy the middle layer; and the bottom layer is savoury, with sandwiches, quiche and sausage rolls.

The fun thing about afternoon tea is that wherever you have it, it will be served differently, and you can really make it your own. If you'd like to use the recipes from this book, here are our suggestions:

- Scones with clotted cream and strawberry jam
- Tuna sandwiches using Tuna Melt filling and cucumber (see page 48)
- Sandwiches with gammon from the rotisserie (see page 68)
- Impossible Quiche (see page 30)
- Sausage Rolls (see page 202)
- Raspberry and White Chocolate Muffins (see page 207)
- Sprinkle Cake (see page 212)
- Three-Ingredient Shortbread (see page 214)

01 Put the flour, sugar, lemonade and yoghurt into a mixing bowl, and mix well with a wooden spoon. Stir in the raisins, then use your hands to bring everything together into a dough. We find it easier to flour our hands when handling the dough.

02 Tip the dough onto a lightly floured worktop and knead lightly until smooth, then shape the dough with your hands, pressing it out until you have a sheet that is 2.5cm/1 inch thick. Use an 8cm/3¼ inch cookie cutter to stamp out circles of dough circles. Gather up your dough leftovers, knead back together and cut again until you have six scones.

03 Place the scones into the air fryer and brush the tops with egg wash. If you are using a basket air fryer, you will need to cook them in batches, but you should be able to fit three in each dual drawer and four in an air fryer basket.

04 Set the temperature to 180°C/360°F and cook for 14 minutes, or until the scones are golden outside and not doughy in the middle.

index

thank you

Wow, another air fryer book! Well, this couldn't have happened without all the amazing people who bought our first book, told their friends about it, wrote amazing reviews, bought extra copies for Christmas presents and continuously spread the word. You are our heroes and we thank you from the bottom of our hearts.

This book is a community effort and we love how your genuine feedback has shaped it. A special shout out to Sue for your support; as requested, we made you smoked haddock. To Pat, for our long-term friendship and shared love of the air fryer oven. To Allan, who asked for some chicken flavouring ideas: you were our inspiration for the seven marinades on page 37.

To our agent Clare, who continues to support us through our passion for the air fryer.

A special mention to the incredible team who produced this book: to our publisher, Denise, who always makes us think outside the box and takes our ideas to the next level; to our photographer Dan; to Becci for your beautiful food styling and awesome editing; to Nicky for your attention to detail; to Faye for your beautiful props (our favourite is the salad bowl used in the autumn salad bowl – it's so pretty); to Georgie for another beautiful design – I am amazed by how you managed to squeeze so much great content into the pages; and, finally, to Liz for her marketing know-how – we just love working with you, and we have made another great book for your mum!

To the ladies of the Inspiring Mums in Business network, who motivated me to make another book and grow our business. I love you all and the amazing businesses we are all building with each other's support. Special mention to Julie, Leanne, Kelly, Kirsty, Jayne, Alison, Tracy and Linda.

To Saskia, for your amazing Tuesday night baking classes. We look forward to them each week and love the invaluable baking skills you are teaching Sofia and Jorge. They loved recreating your flatbread for the cookbook.

To Mrs Gallagher, the best teacher I ever had. Everyone has that one amazing teacher who is remembered for years to come: that is you! I hope you like this book as much as you liked the first!

To Sarah, for your loyal friendship and your commitment to all the recipe testing. We loved your sprinkle cake adaptation the most!

To Kyle, Sofia and Jorge: you're our biggest fans and we are your biggest fans. Mum and dad are incredibly proud of the three of you and all your amazing help. Although, we are sorry to disappoint: the mac and cheese is now fully tested so no more eating mac and cheese for breakfast!

To Kath, you're doing an amazing job learning the air fryer and thank you for your years of support and friendship.

To all our suppliers: Andy and the team at Rafters of Driffield; Daniel at Elston Butchers, the butchers at Vanessa's; and the team at The Refill Jar. You have supplied us with some amazing local produce in the making of this book and it's a pleasure to shop local.

To Claire, Pete, our parents and other family and friends, for your continued support.

about the authors

Sam and Dom Milner have been air frying since 2012 and couldn't imagine day-to-day cooking without the air fryer and their other kitchen gadgets.

In late 2015, they started *Recipe This* so that they could share their love for the air fryer with others and help air-fryer beginners. They are now loved around the world for their air fryer recipes and advice.

They live in Yorkshire in the North of England with their kids Kyle, Sofia and Jorge – and three air fryer ovens, three air fryer baskets and two air fryer duals.

RecipeThis.com